STUDIES
IN
HEBREWS

Books by M. R. De Haan

Adventures in Faith
Bread for Each Day
Broken Things
The Chemistry of the Blood
Coming Events in Prophecy
Daniel the Prophet
The Days of Noah
Dear Doctor: I Have a Problem
508 Answers to Bible Questions
Genesis and Evolution
Studies in Hebrews
The Jew and Palestine in Prophecy
Studies in Jonah
Law or Grace
Our Daily Bread
Pentecost and After
Portraits of Christ in Genesis
Studies in Revelation
The Romance of Redemption
The Second Coming of Jesus
Signs of the Times
Simon Peter
Studies in First Corinthians
Studies in Galatians
The Tabernacle

M. R. De Haan Classic Library

STUDIES IN HEBREWS

M. R. DE HAAN

kregel
PUBLICATIONS

Grand Rapids, MI 49501

Library of Congress Cataloging-in-Publication Data
De Haan, M. R. (Martin Ralph), 1891–1964.
    Studies in Hebrews / M. R. De Haan.
        p.   cm.
    Originally published: Grand Rapids, Mich.: Zondervan Publishing House, 1959.
    1. Bible. N.T. Hebrews—Criticism, interpretation, etc.
I. Title. II. Series: De Haan, M. R. (Martin Ralph), 1891–
1964. M. R. De Haan classic library.
BS2775.2.D44   1996   227'.8706—dc20   96-10315
                                                                                        CIP
ISBN 0-8254-2479-8

                1 2 3 4 5 printing/year 00 99 98 97 96

Printed in the United States of America

Dedication

*To that host of believers who long for
a greater power in Christian service,
and are seeking the maximum of
victory over self and sin, willing to
present their bodies a living sacrifice to
God, this volume is prayerfully dedicated.*

Contents

Foreword

FOR years I have not been satisfied with the general interpretations given of Hebrews six and ten, which chapters seem to be of a highly controversial nature. Then one day it was my privilege to talk to my dearly beloved friend, Dr. M. R. DeHaan, about the interpretation of these two chapters; and his analysis as he gave it to me then, encouraged my own thinking along the same line.

I have read, with great interest, the manuscript of our brother on the Book of Hebrews, in which I believe he sets forth clearly, distinctly and thought-provokingly, an analysis of the book to which all of us should take heed.

Could it be that we have dodged the clear teaching of the Judgment Seat of Christ, because some have taught concerning it that it is some sort of purgatory? Frankly, I have had the word "purgatory" thrown in my face numerous times when setting forth what the Scriptures teach on the subject of the Judgment Seat of Christ.

But the extreme position held by some is no reason for us to back off and ignore the subject. I feel that the correct view of the Judgment Seat of Christ is the basis for purification among God's people, and a teaching which needs to be emphasized.

I am happy for this dissertation on Hebrews, setting forth clearly this all-important doctrine of God's discipline of His children. I believe the right understanding of this subject will give us a right understanding of the appearing of the Lord Jesus Christ, which in turn will make I John 3:3 a much more weighty verse. I quote, "And every man that hath this hope in him purifieth himself, even as he is pure." I am praying that this book will be instrumental in opening the eyes of many wayward Christians, causing them to prepare in the right sense for the return of the Lord Jesus Christ.

THEODORE H. EPP, *Director,*
Back to the Bible Broadcast

Preface

THIS volume is not designed to be an exhaustive exposition of the Book of Hebrews. Instead, it is intended to be an overall view of the central teaching of the book. The heart of this epistle and the key to its correct interpretation we believe is found in chapter five.

> For when for the time ye ought to be teachers, ye have need that one teach you again which be the first principles of the oracles of God; and are become such as have need of milk, and not of strong meat.
> For every one that useth milk is unskilful in the word of righteousness: for he is a babe.
> But strong meat belongeth to them that are of full age, even those who by reason of use have their senses exercised to discern both good and evil (Heb. 5:12-14).

These Hebrew Christians had stopped short of a victorious and fruitful life, and were sorely tempted to become legalistic and to neglect their salvation. They are, therefore, admonished to "go on to perfection" (maturity), lest they harden their hearts and come to a place where it is impossible for them to be renewed again unto repentance, but become unfruitful castaways to suffer loss at the Judgment Seat of Christ. To prevent this from happening, the writer reminds them of the sacrifice of Christ in their behalf, of the presence of the High Priest in heaven, and the power of the solid meat of the Word to enable them to gain the victory and the crown. If this does not induce them to a yielding and surrender to His will, He warns them of the chastening which they are inviting, and finally, if chastening is despised, the Lord may judge them by setting them aside, or visiting them with death, to be judged at the Judgment Seat of Christ.

We realize that this interpretation is not the popular or traditional one, but we have long been convinced that these Hebrews were not mere professors who had gone along with the

Spirit to the very threshold of salvation, and then had gone back before they were actually saved. The description of these Hebrews indicates they were truly born again, and the fruits they had borne in the past classify them as genuine believers. To apply to ourselves those portions of the epistle which speak of the blessings, and then apply the judgments (Heb. 6 and 10) to the poor Hebrews is just as inconsistent as to apply the glorious prophecies of Israel's future glory and restoration in the Old Testament to the Church, and leave the judgments and curses for poor Israel. We believe the Book of Hebrews is written for and to believers, to remind all of us that GRACE carries responsibilities and we cannot live loose, carnal, unseparated lives and expect to escape the results when "the Lord shall judge his people." The background of Hebrews is the Judgment Seat of Christ.

These messages were first given over two coast-to-coast networks of radio stations, and are reproduced much as they were given at that time. They cover only the mountain peaks of Hebrews and the main theme, and are not meant to be an exhaustive treatment of this important book. If reading this volume causes you to turn to the Book of Hebrews, and prompts you to restudy it, even if it be for the purpose of refuting the foregoing interpretation, we shall be grateful. If it drives you to the Word to see if these things are so, then, whether we agree or not, it will be a blessing. We need not all agree, but if we disagree, let us not be disagreeable in our disagreements. With a prayer that these studies may stimulate us all to "search the Scriptures," in a sincere desire to know His will, we send forth this volume.

> That we henceforth be no more children, tossed to and fro, and carried about with every wind of doctrine, by the sleight of men, and cunning craftiness, whereby they lie in wait to deceive;
> But speaking the truth in love, may grow up into him in all things, which is the head, even Christ (Eph. 4:14, 15).

M. R. DeHaan

Grand Rapids, Michigan

STUDIES
IN
HEBREWS

CHAPTER ONE

Saved—or Half Saved

> God, who at sundry times and in divers manners spake in time past unto the fathers by the prophets,
>
> Hath in these last days spoken unto us by his Son, whom he hath appointed heir of all things, by whom also he made the worlds;
>
> Who being the brightness of his glory, and the express image of his person, and upholding all things by the word of his power, when he had by himself purged our sins, sat down on the right hand of the Majesty on high (Heb. 1:1-3).

IN these three verses the Holy Spirit introduces the Book of Hebrews and its inexhaustible treasure of divine revelation concerning Jesus Christ, the Son of God and Son of Man, Creator and Sustainer of the universe, the Saviour of the world, the Purger of our sins, the rightful Heir of all things and the coming eternal King, now seated at the right hand of the Majesty on high.

To write another book on the Epistle to the Hebrews seems upon first thought almost a waste of time and energy, as already so many excellent books have been written on the subject. However, for years I felt the urge to put into print something of the blessing this book has been to me personally, but always I was deterred by the fact that many books had been published on the subject and another volume would only be a repetition. However, the urge persisted, until finally I submitted, in the consciousness that nothing in the Bible can be repeated too often. Instead of a verse-by-verse exposition, it is our purpose to merely give a series of messages on the principal passages, in order to develop the main message of the epistle. Details will, insofar as possible, be avoided, and instead we shall try to bring out the one great lesson of the book — the ministry of Christ as our interceding High Priest, Sustainer and Lord.

MANY THINGS NOT REVEALED

Hebrews is a unique book, quite unlike most books of the Bible. We meet with many questions we shall not even endeavor to answer. For instance, we do not know who the human author was through whom the Holy Spirit spoke. Volumes have been written on the subject, "Who wrote Hebrews?", but no one can speak with finality on the subject. So we pass this by without further comment, satisfied that the Holy Spirit was the divine Author. Neither do we know the exact date of its writing, nor the particular local assembly to whom it was addressed, nor from what place the epistle was written. So there is no need to speculate, since only the message of the book is really important.

The subject of the book is Jesus Christ. It is called the Book of Hebrews simply because the Early Church was at first exclusively composed of Hebrew Christians, and up to the time of Paul still predominantly so. Hence it was written to Hebrew believers and thus it obtained its name. But just exactly who are in the mind of the writer when he addresses them as brethren? This question is not so easily answered. There are at least two views.

First, there are those who teach that Hebrews was written to born-again believers, saved people, warning them of the danger of again falling from grace and finally losing their salvation which they now possessed. This is the view held by the Arminian school of theologians. It is mainly based on chapters six and ten, the two chapters on which most of the difference of opinion and interpretation exists.

A second school of interpretation teaches that the people addressed in the letter were not truly born-again believers, but merely professing Christians, who had come only part way to Christ and were in danger of drawing back before they were finally and actually saved. This is the generally accepted view of the Calvinistic school of interpretation. As an example we quote from the notes on Hebrews six, as given by a well-known exponent of this interpretation.* He states in the following words this most widely accepted position:

> Hebrews 6:4-8 presents the case of Jewish professed believers who halt short of faith in Christ after advancing to the very threshold of salvation, even "going along with" the Holy Spirit in His work of enlightenment and conviction. It is not said that they had faith. This supposed person is like the spies at Kadesh-barnea who saw the land and had the very fruit of it in their hands, and yet turned back.

This interpretation has been generally followed by the great majority of expositors who hold the Calvinistic view of salvation. Now which of these two is correct? They cannot both be right. We confidently believe there need be no doubt concerning the teaching of the Word if we can but approach it with an unprejudiced and unbiased mind, and limit ourselves strictly to the Word and not what others have taught before us.

Who Are They?

We can answer the question satisfactorily only if we consider the teaching of Hebrews in its entirety, and not base our views on isolated passages. One simply cannot know the correct interpretation of Hebrews six and ten without viewing these chapters in the light of the whole epistle. The correct interpretation of the book hinges on the answer to this one question, Were the people addressed Christians or unbelievers, saved or lost? A person cannot be half saved. He is either one or the other. To say they were *partly* saved is to becloud the entire issue. Were these Hebrews saved? From the beginning to the end of Hebrews we sincerely believe that the people to whom the Letter was written were genuine, born-again, saved individuals. The writer identifies himself again and again with those to whom he is writing. The pronoun, "we," which in-

* *Scofield Reference Bible*, p. 1295.

cludes himself, is used over two dozen times, as well as the pronoun, "us." Moreover, the description of these Hebrews is one which can only fit believers.

Notice just a few examples, which we shall elaborate upon later. How can the following passage be made to mean an unregenerate professor?

> Wherefore, holy brethren, partakers of the heavenly calling, consider the Apostle and High Priest of our profession [confession] Christ Jesus (Heb. 3:1).

Can we say this is a description of an unregenerate man? Are unregenerate sinners partakers of the heavenly calling? Is Christ their High Priest, when they have not even received Him as their Saviour? Or consider another passage:

> Seeing then that we have a great high priest, that is passed into the heavens, Jesus the Son of God, let us hold fast our profession (Heb. 4:14).

Are these people addressed unconverted, unregenerated Hebrews who have not been fully saved? A person cannot be "half saved" and "half lost." It is either one or the other. Which are they? If they are false professors, would the Holy Spirit admonish them to hold fast their *false* profession?

Or consider this verse in Hebrews 4:16. Can this be said to an unsaved person:

> Let us therefore come boldly unto the throne of grace.

The sinner cannot come to the Throne of Grace until he comes first to the Cross of Calvary.

Or listen to this passage and tell me whether these people addressed are saved or not. I have never heard a Bible teacher who did not apply this passage to believers:

> Having therefore, brethren, boldness to enter into the holiest by the blood of Jesus,
> By a new and living way, which he hath consecrated for us, through the veil, that is to say, his flesh;
> And having an high priest over the house of God;
> Let us draw near with a true heart in full assurance of faith,

> having our hearts sprinkled from an evil conscience, and our bodies washed with pure water.
>
> Let us hold fast the profession of our faith without wavering; (for he is faithful that promised;)
>
> And let us consider one another to provoke unto love and to good works:
>
> Not forsaking the assembling of ourselves together, as the manner of some is; but exhorting one another: and so much the more, as ye see the day approaching (Heb. 10:19-25).

Is this admonition to believers or sinners? Does God urge an unconverted, half-saved professor to hold fast his false profession? Every author I have ever read on the subject agrees that this is addressed to believers. It is incontrovertible. By what rule of interpretation can we then say that the very next verse is addressed not to believers but to false professors?

> For if we sin wilfully after that we have received the knowledge of the truth, there remaineth no more sacrifice for sins (Heb. 10:26).

"For if *we* sin wilfully." Who are the *we?* The same ones who in the previous verses are unmistakably identified as God's children, who are admonished to *hold fast* their profession. The twenty-sixth verse continues without a break, connected with the preceding verses by the word "for." "*For if we sin wilfully ....*" The way to avoid willful sinning is for the believer to *hold fast his profession.*

We give just one more example. Another portion of Hebrews mentions the people who are warned against willful sinning:

> For ye had compassion of me in my bonds, and took joyfully the spoiling of your goods, knowing in yourselves that ye have in heaven a better and an enduring substance.
>
> Cast not away therefore your confidence, which hath great recompence of reward (Heb. 10:34, 35).

This last word *reward* is the key which unlocks the secret of the Book of Hebrews. It is not written to half-saved professors who are threatened with being lost after all. Instead it is written to believers who *are saved* and *cannot be lost* again, but

they can lose their *reward*. The warning is to believers coming
short of God's best, and becoming subject to the chastening of
the Lord, and loss of reward at the Judgment Seat of Christ.
These Hebrews knew they had in heaven a better and more
enduring substance, and were admonished by the Holy Spirit
to *hold fast* their confidence.

<h3 style="text-align:center">THE HEART OF HEBREWS</h3>

The very heart of the Book of Hebrews, therefore, is a solemn
plea to believers not to be satisfied with mere salvation or anything less than the best and the very maximum of fruit and
service. It teaches that we are saved by grace and grace alone,
but that this grace also carries with it serious responsibilities.
Works have no part in salvation by grace, but works are an es-
sential result of grace. Because we *are* saved by grace, the
Lord expects of us that we shall bring forth the fruits of grace.
We are not to stand still and be merely satisfied with being
saved from hell and headed for heaven, but we are to become
mature and fruitful in our Christian life. These Hebrews are
warned not to remain children in the faith, but to grow up.
As Peter puts it:

> Grow in grace, and in the knowledge of our Lord and Saviour
> Jesus Christ (II Pet. 3:18).

It is not grow *into* grace, but grow *in* grace. The very heart
of Hebrews, the key to its right interpretation, is found in chapter five.

> For when for the time ye ought to be teachers [considering
> the length of time they had been saved], ye have need that one
> teach you again which be the first principles of the oracles of
> God; and are become such as have need of milk, and not of strong
> meat.
> For every one that useth milk is unskilful in the word of
> righteousness: for he is a babe.
> But strong meat belongeth to them that are of full age [mature,
> grown up], even those who by reason of use have their senses ex-
> ercised to discern both good and evil (Heb. 5:12-14).

These Christians had been saved a long time but were still babes in Christ, and could not take the solid meat of the Word, and so they were admonished to grow up. The Holy Spirit continues:

> Therefore leaving the principles of the doctrine of Christ, let *us* go on unto perfection [maturity, full age] (Heb. 6:1).

Failure to heed the admonition will result in the chastening of the Lord. Continuance in this state of arrested spiritual development, persisting in living in disobedience, will not go unjudged, but will surely be judged of the Lord. If, after repeated warnings and chastening of the Lord such a believer still persists in his carnality, then God may punish that believer by physical death, or cease dealing with him, to become a "castaway" (I Cor. 9:27), to be judged at the Judgment Seat of Christ, where he will *suffer* loss but be saved so as by fire (I Cor. 3:15). This is the penalty for the "sin unto death" (I John 5:16), called in Hebrews "willful sinning." If the believer, after being enlightened, having tasted the heavenly gift, and being partaker of the Holy Ghost, having tasted the good Word of God and the powers of the world to come, refuses to go on but "falls away," God may cease to deal with him in repentance, and reserve him for the fires of the Judgment Seat of Christ.

GOD WILL JUDGE HIS PEOPLE

Are you a believer? Have you received Jesus Christ as your personal Saviour by grace? Then comes the question, What have you done with that grace of God? Have you gone on to maturity? Has there been a growth in grace? Are you living an obedient life in holiness and separation from the world? Or are you continuing in carnality and willful sinning against the clear teaching and better knowledge of the Word of God? Are you clinging to some sin you know is contrary to God's Word? Do you condone and excuse certain things in your life which you know are wrong? You'll never get away with it.

The Lord shall judge his people (Heb. 10:30).

We cannot escape the fact that sin in the life of the believer must be judged if unconfessed. We can try to get around it by saying that the warnings of Hebrews six and ten are for unsaved people, half-saved Hebrews, and do not apply to us. God will also judge such handling of the Scriptures in our effort to avoid the application of the words of Hebrews 10:31:

> It is a fearful thing to fall into the hands of the living God.

The lesson and burden of the Book of Hebrews is not salvation for sinners primarily, but it has to do with rewards or loss of rewards for believers at the Judgment Seat of Christ. We cannot escape it by applying it to others, but the rather, let us heed the admonition in Hebrews 12:1, 2:

> . . . let us lay aside every weight, and the sin which doth so easily beset us, and let us run with patience the race that is set before us,
> Looking unto Jesus the author and finisher of our faith . . . .

Let it never be said of us:

> And ye have forgotten the exhortation which speaketh unto you as unto children, My son, despise not thou the chastening of the Lord, nor faint when thou art rebuked of him (Heb. 12:5).

Let us examine our hearts for every known and doubtful sin, and when we can find no more, then ask of Him:

> Search me, O God, and know my heart: try me, and know my thoughts:
> And see if there be any wicked way in me, and lead me in the way everlasting (Ps. 139:23, 24).

CHAPTER TWO

Neglecting Our Salvation

THE Book of Hebrews was written to born-again believers who are admonished not to stop short of God's best in a life of holiness, service and fruit bearing. He has provided everything for our growth in grace and expects us to develop into spiritual maturity. He Himself has made adequate provision whereby this may be attained, for Christ is at the right hand of God as our pleading High Priest, ever living to intercede for us. There is no excuse for any Christian remaining a spiritual babe, or living a defeated life, or being unfruitful because of His provision and also because:

> . . . we have a great high priest, that is passed into the heavens, Jesus the Son of God, let us hold fast our profession.
> For we have not an high priest which cannot be touched with the feeling of our infirmities; but was in all points tempted like as we are, yet without sin (Heb. 4:14, 15).

This is God's provision for our weakness and failure. Jesus Christ our High Priest understands all our struggles, temptations and trials, and is waiting only for the discouraged and defeated child of God to come to Him and draw upon His mercy and grace for victory, and so chapter four of Hebrews closes with:

> Let us therefore come boldly unto the throne of grace, that we may obtain mercy [forgiveness for past failures], and find grace to help in time of need [provision for future victory] (Heb. 4:16).

With this adequate provision there is no excuse for the child of God to continue in defeat, or disobedience to His command,

23

"Let us go on unto perfection" [maturity] (Heb. 6:1). To continue in unrepentance and to condone evil in our lives constitutes willful sinning, the sin unto death, and will be judged of the Lord either here in chastening, or at the Judgment Seat of Christ to suffer loss. This we believe to be the message of the Book of Hebrews.

The Person of the Book

The Book of Hebrews opens with a portrait of the Lord Jesus Christ as the eternal Son of God and Saviour of men. Jesus is not only a new Testament character, but is also the God of the Old Testament. The Jehovah of the Old Testament is the Jesus Christ of the New. This is settled for us in the opening verses:

> God, who at sundry times and in divers manners spake in time past unto the fathers by the prophets,
> Hath in these last days [latter times] spoken unto us by his Son (Heb. 1:1, 2).

That this Son is very God, and one with the Father is then immediately asserted by a number of divine characteristics.

1. He is the Heir of all things (v. 2).
2. He is the Creator of the universe (v. 2).
3. He is the brightness of the glory of God (v. 3.)
4. He is of the same substance (v. 3).
5. He is the Sustainer of the universe (v. 3).
6. He is the sinless Purger of others' sins (v. 3).
7. He is sitting upon the throne of Deity (v. 3).

Here are seven things said of the Son in the first three verses of chapter one, which cannot be said of any created being, but only of Deity. If there were no other passage in the Bible setting forth the Deity of Jesus Christ, these first three verses of Hebrews would be all-sufficient. Thus the subject of Hebrews is introduced as Jesus, the Son of God.

In His Humanity

This eternal God, however, became a man, took on Him a human nature, "being made in fashion as a man." John says, "The Word became flesh." Did He then cease to be God when He became a man? Did He lay aside His Deity at his humiliation? If He did, how then could He ever become God again? Is Jesus Christ, the man in the glory, still one with God the Father and the Holy Spirit? This is the issue the writer next takes up. Even in His humanity He is still above all other created beings. He is better than the angels.

> Being made so much better than the angels, as he hath by inheritance received a more excellent name than they.
> For unto which of the angels said he at any time, Thou art my Son, this day have I begotten thee? (Heb. 1:4, 5).

The elect angels of God are the highest order of all created beings. They never fell by sin, they have access to the very presence of God, they are entrusted with the most weighty and responsible tasks, they are God's messengers and executors of His will. There are no created beings above them, and they take orders from no one but God. And Christ is said to be better than the angels — therefore, He is God, for there is none better than the angels except God. To further emphasize the superlative excellency of Jesus as the Son of God even while in human form and in the body of His humiliation, the book continues:

> And again, when he bringeth in the firstbegotten into the world, he saith, And let all the angels of God worship him (Heb. 1:6).

God had said, "Thou shalt worship the Lord thy God and him only shalt thou serve." By accepting worship, Jesus is declared to be God. All these things are true of Jesus as a man, dwelling in human flesh and with a human nature. This is evident, for it says he was *made* better than the angels. The angels are told to worship Him when the Firstbegotten was brought into the world. Now the force of all this is that the One who hung upon the Cross of Calvary covered with blood and spittle, meekly suffering the very acme of insult and humiliation was none other than Almighty God, the Creator, being crucified by His creatures. Only as we bear in mind who He was can we understand the demand of the Book of Hebrews that the redeemed go on to perfection, and not stop short of complete dedication to Him. This, we repeat, is the message of Hebrews, a plea to believers to yield their all to Him who is so graphically described as the Son of God and the Son of Man.

The balance of chapter one is an ever-mounting cumulative argument for the superiority of Christ over the angelic host. Remembering that those to whom the epistle was addressed were Hebrew Christians who had the greatest and deepest reverence for the angels of God, the argument would be most convincing. The contrast with the angels is striking. Of the Son of God it is said:

1. He is a King in His Kingdom (v. 8).
2. He is the sinless One (v. 9).
3. He is the Designer of the universe (v. 10).
4. He is the eternal Creator (v. 11).
5. He is unchangeable (v. 12).
6. He is the final Conqueror (v. 13).
7. He is the Lord of angels (v. 14).

None — not one of these can be said of the highest angels.

THEREFORE! WHEREFORE?

No great wonder that the next chapter opens with the admonition:

> Therefore we ought to give the more earnest heed to the things which we have heard, lest at any time we should let them slip.
> For if the word spoken by angels was stedfast, and every transgression and disobedience received a just recompence of reward;
> How shall we escape, if we neglect so great salvation (Heb. 2:1-3).

THEREFORE! WHEREFORE?

Two things in these verses are to be noted. They are the first word, "therefore," and then the repeated use of the pronoun, "we." He is addressing believers and classes himself with them, saying, "Therefore *we* ought to give heed to what *we* have heard, lest *we* should let these things slip." And then he warns, "How shall *we* escape if *we* neglect so great salvation?" The meaning becomes clear when we remember the teaching of chapter one. The Lord Jesus is presented in His superlative excellency as Creator, Sustainer, Saviour and Intercessor. In view of all that He is, and all He has done for us, He has a right to claim our absolute devotion and obedience, the maximum of service and fruit bearing. That is the force of the word, "therefore." It demands a "wherefore?" It is because of what He has done for us by His grace that He has a right to expect unquestioning obedience to His claims. Therefore, because of this, "we ought to give the more earnest heed . . . lest . . . we should let them slip." The writer is not talking about losing salvation. Neither is he speaking to unconverted professing Hebrews, for he would not admonish them to hold fast and not let slip a false profession. He is speaking of our service and rewards. This is made clear by the warning:

> How shall we escape, if we neglect so great salvation (Heb. 2:3).

NEGLECT — NOT REJECT

This text is almost universally applied to the sinner and used for an evangelistic sermon. As an application this may be justified, but the interpretation applies to the saint — not the sinner. Two words hold the key, the words "we" and "neglect." The "we" implies that he is addressing believers. The word "neglect" assumes that we already possess something which may be neglected. The text does not say, "How shall we escape if we *reject* so great salvation?" These Hebrew Christians had not *rejected* the Gospel, but had *received* this great salvation. They were saved, justified and secure by free grace, but now works

must follow. We must *do* something with our salvation, and
because we are saved, it must not be neglected. Conversion is
not the end of our salvation, but the beginning. We must go
on to perfection. This is the goal and theme of the entire epistle.
Israel was out of Egypt, redeemed by the blood, but the goal
was Canaan, the land of victory. Yet only a few reached this
fruitful land. The great host, though delivered by the blood,
and never to return to Egypt, died in the wilderness and failed
to reach the land of victory. Canaan is not heaven, but stands
for victory here and now, the very thing the Book of Hebrews
sets forth.

WORK OUT YOUR SALVATION

The Apostle Paul, writing to the Philippians says:

> Wherefore, my beloved, as ye have always obeyed, not as in
> my presence only, but now much more in my absence, work out
> your own salvation with fear and trembling (Phil. 2:12).

This is addressed to believers who *are* saved. He calls them
"beloved." It deals with obedience. They were not to work *for*
salvation, but to *work out* their salvation. God works it *in;* we
work it out. Salvation is a gift, but it carries responsibilities.
We can make it produce fruit, or it can be neglected. To illustrate: Suppose I give you a farm as a gift. It cost you not a
cent. It is delivered to you free and clear. You are given a war-
ranty deed. It is yours. Now you can work that farm diligently
and make it productive, or you can neglect it. Your neglect will
not forfeit your title to the farm, but it will deprive you of the
blessing and reward of your labor. So too with salvation. It
is a free gift by grace, but your reward or loss at the harvest time
depends on what you work *out* of your salvation. There is an
accounting coming, and God will judge every believer on the
basis of what he has done with the opportunities, time and responsibilities of salvation. This will occur at the Judgment Seat
of Christ. The word is clear:

> For we must all appear before the judgment seat of Christ; that
> every one may receive the things done in his body, according to
> that he hath done, whether it be good or bad (II Cor. 5:10).

GOOD OR BAD

The reward at the Judgment Seat will be for those whose record is good, and those who have neglected their great salvation "will suffer loss." This we believe to be the meaning of Hebrews 2:3,

> How shall we escape, if we neglect so great salvation.

Escape what? Not hell, for escaping hell is by grace — not works. It is escaping God's disapproval at the time of reckoning. Listen again to Paul:

> Every man's work shall be made manifest: for the day shall declare it, because it shall be revealed by fire; and the fire shall try every man's work of what sort it is.
>
> If any man's work abide which he hath built thereupon, he shall receive a reward.
>
> If any man's work shall be burned, he shall suffer loss: but he himself shall be saved; yet so as by fire (I Cor. 3:13-15).

These indeed are solemn words. Just because we are saved this does not mean we can live as we please and do as we wish. Grace does not give a license to sin or constitute an excuse for carelessness. We must all appear before the Judgment Seat of Christ to answer for the things done after we are saved. In view of this clear revelation of God, we can appreciate the solemn warning of Hebrews:

> Therefore we ought to give the more earnest heed to the things which we have heard . . . .
>
> How shall we escape, if we neglect so great salvation (Heb. 2:1, 3).

This is the message of Hebrews so sadly overlooked. Thousands of Christians need to learn the lesson that conversion is only the first step in a process which will only be completed when we are perfectly and completely conformed to the image of Jesus. God will not cease to deal with us until we are brought to the maturity of our growth in grace and knowledge of the Lord Jesus.

The Demands of Grace

Until we realize that God expects us to bring forth the maximum of fruit, by complete obedience to His will, practical separation from the world and a full surrender of our whole being, we will remain infants in the faith, defeated and fruitless. Have you neglected your great salvation? How long have you been saved? How much progress have you made? Is your Christian service a joy and a challenge? Do you bear the burdens of life without murmuring? Do you have the full assurance of salvation? If Jesus should call you home today, could you meet Him with confidence? Why not take a step forward today? Stop and take careful inventory of your progress, and honestly confess the things you know are hindering you in your testimony, service and assurance. Then come in repentance, ask His forgiveness, claim the promises, and yield your life to Him. Listen to the admonition of John:

> And now, little children, abide in him; that, when he shall appear, we may have confidence, and not be ashamed before him at his coming (I John 2:28).

I can imagine someone saying, Yes, that is my desire. I am tired of this life of defeat. How may I become victorious and go on to perfection? Hebrews twelve gives the answer:

> Wherefore seeing we also are compassed about with so great a cloud of witnesses, let us lay aside every weight, and the sin which doth so easily beset us, and let us run with patience the race that is set before us,
> Looking unto Jesus the author and finisher of our faith; who for the joy that was set before him endured the cross, despising the shame, and is set down at the right hand of the throne of God (Heb. 12:1.2).

There is the pattern. First, judge every known and doubtful sin in your life, the weights that hold you down, the sins which beset you. Confess them and accept His forgiveness. Next, fix your eyes only on Jesus. Get your eyes off self and others. Interpret every experience of life, not in terms of the present sacrifice of suffering, but in terms of future glory. Jesus is our

Example, who for the joy *ahead*, endured the Cross without murmuring, and despised the shame (we only endure the shame) and is today exalted on high as the High Priest, waiting to help you to follow in His footsteps.

Don't look back and cry over spilt milk. Don't interpret any experience in terms of today, but translate all of them into terms of eternity. Remember,

> . . . no chastening for the present seemeth to be joyous, but grievous: nevertheless afterward it yieldeth the peaceable fruit of righteousness unto them which are exercised thereby.
>
> Wherefore lift up the hands which hang down [put your idle hands to work], and the feeble knees [quit stumbling]:
>
> And make straight paths for your feet [begin walking—don't just stand there] (Heb. 12:11-13).

Go on, go on, start walking. And keep your eyes on Jesus. Don't look to the right or the left, nor behind you, but keep your eye on the goal, and your feet will grow wings beneath you.

CHAPTER THREE

The Goal of Salvation

> Thou madest him a little lower than the angels; thou crownedst him with glory and honour, and didst set him over the works of thy hands:
> Thou hast put all things in subjection under his feet (Heb. 2:7, 8).

THE Epistle to the Hebrews was addressed to believers in the early apostolic Church who were almost entirely converts from Judaism, who had been saved out of a religion of law works, based on a corrupted, distorted system of superstition and tradition as taught by the apostate priesthood and Pharisees of that day. What this corrupted religion was, and what Jesus thought of it may be seen by reading Matthew twenty-three. These Hebrew Christians had only recently come out of this environment into the unpopular fellowship of a new sect of believers called Christians. To take a firm, uncompromising stand for the truth of the Gospel was for them not an easy matter. It meant giving up friends, parting with dear ones, breaking with their old religious system, and walking the lonely path of separation with Christ and a little company of people who were followers of the despised Nazarene. It meant giving up things they had held dear, and invoking the ridicule of the religious elite of that day, and even inviting persecution.

This was the price which these early Christians had to pay to follow the despised Saviour who Himself had forewarned them of this, and said:

> In the world ye shall have tribulation but be of good cheer; I have overcome the world (John 16:33).

It had been easy for them to accept Christ, for that was a free gift, but to "go on" with Christ was quite another matter. It is no wonder then that many of them weakened along the way, and to avoid persecution and ostracism were tempted to go back into the old legalistic way, and to compromise with the world about them. They had lost their separated position of testimony and taken the easy and popular path of seeking the favor of their old companions and friends. They had begun well, but then somehow they had lost their first love and earnest zeal, and had slumped into a condition of lukewarmness, apathy and fruitlessness. After years of Christian experience they were still babes in Christ, immature infants, suffering from spiritual malnutrition, going backward instead of forward. They had walked in the full liberty of grace, and now were going back to the dead works of the law. It was the same situation as with those in Galatia to whom Paul wrote:

O foolish Galatians, who hath bewitched you . . . .
Are ye so foolish? having begun in the Spirit, are ye now made perfect [mature] by the flesh [law]? (Gal. 3:1, 3)

They too had begun in faith, but were tempted to continue in the flesh. It was the subtle error of supposing we are saved by grace, and then kept by the works of the law. The same thing applied to these Hebrew Christians and the entire book is designed to teach them that they are saved by grace, but must continue to gain the ultimate victory by depending on this same grace to enable them to gain the crown through their faithfulness.

We Must Grow Up

The Christian life is a growth in grace, and should never know retreat or standing still. Conversion is only the first step in a long journey to our ultimate goal. When God saves a person, His final goal for that individual is to make him ultimately just like the Lord Jesus in all perfection. Paul tells us in Romans:

For whom he did foreknow, he also did predestinate to be conformed to the image of his Son, that he might be the firstborn
among many brethren (Rom. 8:29).

Salvation is far more than being delivered from hell and
going to heaven when we die. These are incidentals and by-
products — bonuses of salvation. His real purpose is to make
perfect saints out of worthless sinners. There are then two possibilities of Christian experience. One is to have salvation,
period; and the other is to have salvation, *plus.* One is to be
just saved by grace; the other is to know a life of power, victory,
joy, service and fruitfulness and a reward at the end of the way.
And it all depends on what we do with God's gift of salvation.
We can develop it or neglect it.

We are faced today with a brand of cheap, shallow gospel.
Men are told they have but to believe, accept Jesus Christ,
raise the hand, sign a card, and they are saved. Undoubtedly
many are, but the tragedy is that this seems to be all there
is to it. In too many cases there is no change evident, for the
preaching of separation from the world of sin and evil is sadly
lacking. People claiming to be converted continue right on in
their "shady" dealings, questionable and evil habits. They go
right on with their worldly occupations and associations. They
continue to fellowship with unbelievers, supporting Christ-
denying organizations, and giving their endorsement to those
who deny the faith once for all delivered to the saints. After
conversion they seem to have no sense of duty to separate themselves and come out from among the enemies of Christ. They
still continue the unequal yoke, frequent the same places of
worldly amusement, indulge in the same habits of entertainment. In short, there is nothing in their lives to indicate that
a change has taken place except that they go on Sunday to the
"church of their choice."

God Demands Separation

The Bible, however, is clear that when we receive Christ,
there must be a break with the old life. There cannot be any

compromise, for a compromising Christian can do more damage than an out-and-out infidel. These Hebrew Christians needed to learn this lesson, that they could not follow Jesus and at the same time go back to the works of the law and compromise their testimony. To do so is to remain infants in the faith, and lose out on God's best. The Lord asks of every believer that he shall yield himself fully to His will, and His will is "holiness unto the Lord." How much progress have you made? Looking back over the years of your Christian life, how is your growth? Are you as spiritual, as zealous, as eager to do God's will now as you were those wonderful days right after you were saved? What has happened? Where is that zeal and joy and passion for souls and holy boldness to stand without compromise for Christ? What has happened? Here and there sin came in and gradually you began to slip away from Him. Then the words of Hebrews 2:1 should help you in your diagnosis:

> Therefore we ought to give the more earnest heed to the things which we have heard, lest at any time we should let them slip.

Two Kinds of Christians

There are two kinds of Christians. Paul calls them carnal and spiritual, those who follow men, and those who follow Christ. There are victorious Christians and defeated ones. There are those who have life, and others who have abundant life (John 10:10). Some have the water of life in them (John 4:14); others have it flowing out of them (John 7:38). There are those who have come *to* Christ for salvation (Matt. 11:28), and others who have learned to follow *after* Him, to take up His yoke of service and obedience, and to be in absolute subjection to His will (Matt. 11:29). Those who have made the surrender and yielded their lives are in a minority, but they are the only ones God uses to any degree. Almost every servant of God whom God has used in any degree has had two calls; one to come to Him for salvation; and another to yield his life in full surrender to His will. This is the life "more abundantly."

God demands this sacrifice and obedience, if we are to know

the joy of service. Listen to God's pleading in His Word for
this life of separation:

> That ye may be blameless and harmless, the sons of God, with-
> out rebuke, in the midst of a crooked and perverse nation, among
> whom ye shine as lights in the world:
> Holding forth the word of life (Phil. 2:15, 16).
>
> See then that ye walk circumspectly, not as fools, but as wise,
> Redeeming the time, because the days are evil (Eph. 5:15, 16).
>
> That we henceforth be no more children, tossed to and fro,
> and carried about with every wind of doctrine . . .
>
> But speaking the truth in love, may grow up into him in all
> things, which is the head, even Christ (Eph. 4:14, 15).

This is God's will for every believer, and to come short of
it means chastening and loss at the end of the road. The only
walk pleasing to God is a separated walk. Paul pleads with us:

> Be ye not unequally yoked together with unbelievers (II Cor.
> 6:14).
>
> Wherefore come out from among them, and be ye separate,
> saith the Lord, and touch not the unclean thing; and I will re-
> ceive you (II Cor. 6:17).

In II Corinthians Paul pleads with us to

> . . . cleanse ourselves from all filthiness of the flesh and spirit,
> perfecting holiness in the fear of God (II Cor. 7:1).

In passing, notice the two kinds of filthiness from which we
are to purge ourselves. They are filthiness of the "flesh" and
"spirit." All will agree with the first, that there is filthiness of
the flesh. How easily we condemn these sins of the flesh — dishonesty, unchastity, robbery, lying, cursing and the like. But
filthiness of the spirit is the sin of fellowship with the world,
and false religion, and encouraging the unfruitful works of
darkness instead of rebuking them.

Now to return to the Book of Hebrews, we see that this ab-
sence of spiritual progress among these Hebrew Christians was
due to their failure to separate from evil doctrine. They had
slipped back into the bondage of the law. No matter what the
price of obedience may be, they are to ask but one thing, "What

does God require of me?" And this request to follow Jesus all the way, to grow into maturity, is reasonable and just. Three arguments are put forth to induce these Christians to consecrate their all to Him, and not stop short of perfection.

1. The first argument is the tremendous price at which our salvation was purchased. Gratitude for so great a salvation should evince the ready response of every believing heart. "Jesus paid it all; All to Him I owe." In Hebrews 2:5-8 we have an account of the infinite price of our salvation in the Incarnation, Christ being made a little lower than the angels. In verse nine we read:

> We see Jesus, who was made a little lower than the angels for the suffering of death (Heb. 2:9).

How can any believer stand at the manger in Bethlehem and realize that there God emptied Himself to save us, and not be deeply moved? How can we behold Him, covered with blood and spittle in Pilate's hall and realize it was in our place, and not be willing to say, "Take my life and let it be consecrated, Lord, to Thee." How can a truly born-again believer stand at Calvary in the awful stifling darkness, and hear the cry of the Son of God that shook the foundations of heaven, "My God, My God, Why hast Thou forsaken Me?" and not fall down before Him and cry:

> Were the whole realm of nature mine,
> That were a present far too small;
> Love so amazing, so divine,
> Demands my soul, my life, my all.

Yet it is a sad, sad fact, not only among these early Hebrew Christians, but also among us, that so many Christians are not living all-out for Christ, but neglecting this great salvation, and wasting life, time, energy and money which belong to Him, in selfish gratification. And so if the love of Christ will not constrain us, then the Lord adds a second inducement for us to follow Him. And that is:

2. A promise of a reward. The Lord does not have to promise a reward for faithful, obedient service. He owes us nothing —

we owe Him all. He has a perfect right to expect our full and devoted service simply on the basis of His redemption and His love for us. But He knows how hard the path sometimes is, and so He in grace promises something extra for faithful service. But it is still a reward of grace. I have a right to expect of my two sons unquestioning devotion and obedience. I ask them to mow the lawn for me, without excuses. I do not have to pay them. They are my sons. They owe their life to me. I have fed and clothed them and provided for their every need. It is not only reasonable and right, but it should be a joy to do this for their father. But I also know those boys, and realize how hard the work seems at times. Their mind is on playing or romping, and so, just to encourage them and give an added incentive, I promise each one a dollar as a reward. It is not pay or wages, for I owe them nothing. It is a reward of grace.

So too our heavenly Father has a right to expect our very best at all times. But He also knows our frame and remembers that we are dust. He knows the struggle with self and the flesh, and how weary we sometimes become, even in His service, and so He promises a reward, an extra reward for faithfulness. It is not pay, not wages, but grace. How wonderful the thoughtfulness of our faithful High Priest who is touched with the feeling of our infirmities, being in all points tempted as we are, yet without sin.

But sad to say, there are Christians who are not constrained by the love of Christ, nor interested in the reward, but in spite of all, continue in a carnal, selfish, fruitless life. What about such? They are saved, and on the way to heaven, but is there no penalty for their disobedience? Indeed there is. And here is the third inducement to obedience.

3. Continued disobedience is inviting the chastening of the Lord. To correct such the Lord may send sickness, weakness and as a last resort, death. God may cut short one's stay on earth rather than have him continue in disobedience (I Cor. 11:30-32). And then for others who persist in rebellion, there may come a

time when their willful sinning will result in God ceasing to deal with them here, waiting to fully judge them at the Judgment Seat of Christ. Such cannot be renewed again unto repentance (Heb. 6:6), but become God's "castaways" (I Cor. 9:27). They will see all their works burned, and they themselves suffering loss, but will be saved so as by fire. God will not allow abuse of the grace of God to go unpunished. He will have His people clean, and if not here, unrepented sins will be burned out in the fires of the Judgment Seat of Christ (I Cor. 3:13-15).

Oh, take stock, believer, and ask yourself, "Is my life pleasing to God?" Come to Him, and confess and repent and then "go on to perfection," for

How shall we escape, if we neglect so great salvation (Heb. 2:3).

CHAPTER FOUR

Lower than the Angels

Being made so much better than the angels, as he hath by inheritance obtained a more excellent name than they (Heb. 1:4).

But we see Jesus, who was made a little lower than the angels for the suffering of death (Heb. 2:9).

"THE Bible cannot be the infallible word of God because it contradicts itself." This is the charge repeatedly hurled against the Bible by infidels and unbelievers. This should be no surprise to us, for the unbeliever is blind to spiritual things, being devoid of the faith by which only regenerate believers can understand the mystery of the Gospel. The natural man receiveth not the things of the Spirit of God, for they are spiritually discerned. What seems, therefore, to be a contradiction to the unsaved, is the very evidence of divine inspiration to the believer. Critics of the Bible have scoffed, for instance, at the account given by Moses of his own death (Deut. 34:1-8). How could Moses have written this record of his own death and burial after he was dead? But right here we have the best kind of proof of inspiration. Moses was inspired by the Holy Spirit to write his own obituary before he died. It is no different from the inspiration of the prophets who infallibly foretold the future history of Israel and the coming of Messiah centuries before these things occurred.

SON OF GOD — SON OF MAN

As another example of an apparent contradiction we have these two verses in Hebrews. In Hebrews one we see Jesus as the Son of God, the Creator and Sustainer of the universe, the Heir of all things, seated at the right hand of the Majesty on high. He is said to be *better* than the angels. The highest order of created beings is that of the angels of God, attending constantly upon God in the heavens. But in chapter two we have quite another picture of Jesus, not as the sovereign Son of God, but the humiliation of the incarnation of the Son of man, suffering and dying for poor, lost sinners. This constitutes our responsibility to Him. It is the argument of Hebrews that we should hold nothing back in our service to Him, but go on to perfection. This request is based on what He is (the Son of God) and what He did to redeem us as the Son of Man. Man by creation was given a position of honor upon this earth, above the angels. He was made the lord of creation and given complete dominion over the earth. It was God who said:

> Let us make man in our image, after our likeness: and let them have dominion over the fish of the sea, and over the fowl of the air, and over the cattle, and over all the earth, and over every creeping thing that creepeth upon the earth (Gen. 1:26).

This dominion is re-asserted in Genesis 1:28. Man's authority and dominion was absolute and universal over earth, contingent on only one condition — obedience to God. But man ignored God's word, partook of the forbidden fruit and fell. By the fall he lost his dominion over the earth, and instead of being its master, he became the slave of sin, to lose all dominion in death. But God's purpose for which He created man is not to be defeated by the devil, and so He makes a second man, the Last Adam, who is to restore this dominion over the earth to man. This dominion is still future, to be realized when Jesus comes again. Through Him, when He comes, the government of the world will someday be given to God's children, who shall reign with Christ over the earth.

What an honor God has bestowed upon us, an honor denied the angels of God:

> For unto the angels hath he not put in subjection the world to come, whereof we speak (Heb. 2:5).

And then follows a quotation from Psalm eight. David says as he beheld the great universe:

> When I consider thy heavens, the work of thy fingers, the moon and the stars, which thou hast ordained;
> What is man, that thou art mindful of him? and the son of man, that thou visitest him? (Ps. 8:3, 4)

WHAT IS MAN?

David is carried away with wonder, awe and adoration. It was a prophetic utterance. It applies first of all to mankind, who had lost dominion, but would have this dominion once more restored. He looked ahead and saw the redemption of all creation, and man again in authority. Considering this he says prophetically:

> Thou madest him a little lower than the angels; thou crownedst him with glory and honour, and didst set him over the works of thy hands:
> Thou hast put all things in subjection under his feet. For in that he put all in subjection under him, he left nothing that is not put under him (Heb. 2:7, 8).

This is what David saw in the future. The authority which Adam lost was to be returned and restored. Only by faith could this be said, for when David wrote and up to this very time, we see nothing of this at all. Death still reigns supreme, rebellion and ungodliness are rampant, storms and catastrophes are still unconquered, and the world is in bondage to the forces of nature and under the sentence of death. The writer of Hebrews realized this, and so adds:

> But now we see not yet all things put under him (Heb. 2:8b).

ENTER THE SECOND MAN

How then shall this dominion be restored? God had cursed man with death, placed the whole earth under the despoilment of Adam's sin. Since God is holy and cannot overlook sin, some way must be found to remove the cause of man's subjection, and the humiliation of universal death. And with the eye of the prophet, David sees the answer. He saw no signs about him in nature to suggest that man was regaining his dominion over the earth which Adam had lost. But he saw another Man, the Last Adam, who would make this redemption possible by a stupendous plan of God. After therefore confessing, "But now we see not yet all things put under him [man]" (Heb. 2:8b), the author of Hebrews says, *but we see Jesus.*

He saw the answer in another Man, the Second Man, the Last Adam, who would accomplish the restoration of that which the first man had lost by sin. And this redemption was to be accomplished by the Incarnation, whereby God becomes man by a supernatural conception and the virgin birth. God stoops to the level of humanity. This is the force of the words, "But we see Jesus, who was made a little lower than the angels." Of man it was said that he was made a little lower than the angels (Heb. 2:7), but he fell; and now to save him, God sends Christ to become a man, to become a little lower than the angels. What a gulf He spanned — from *"higher than,"* to *"lower than"* the angels. By His birth Jesus identified Himself with Adam's race.

> For verily he took not on him the nature of angels; but he took on him the seed of Abraham (Heb. 2:16).

The purpose of this incarnation was that as a man He might pay man's debt. Notice that it was for the "suffering of death" that He who was crowned with glory and honor became a little lower than the angels and should taste death for every man (2:7). The goal of Jesus becoming a little lower than the angels was the Cross. There the redemption would be consummated. This was all in perfect harmony with the character of Christ. It was just like Him, and in harmony with His great love for them, to do so. Notice how it is stated:

> For it became him, for whom are all things, and by whom are all things, in bringing many sons unto glory, to make the captain of their salvation perfect through sufferings (Heb. 2:10).

It Became Him

The phrase, "it became him," may be translated, "it was becoming on him." We say a hat or a dress is becoming on a person, meaning it fits the personality of the wearer, and it looks good. So the love of Christ in dying for us was becoming to Him, for it exactly fitted and expressed His personality. Nothing else could do. If Jesus is to restore Adam's lost inheritance, it must be by the suffering of death. Again we must be reminded *who* it was, and *who* did all this. It was the One "for whom are all things, and by whom are all things." It was the sovereign Creator, and He was made perfect through sufferings.

Perfect through Sufferings

This is indeed a strange statement, that Christ was made "perfect through sufferings." Was not He perfect God and perfect Man? Certainly, but here we are dealing with Christ as the Redeemer. Without the suffering of death He could not "perfect" our salvation. If Jesus had been unable or unwilling to die in our place, He would be an imperfect Saviour, even though perfect God and Man. But He is perfect in all His attributes and so He proved Himself perfect in His love for us in redeeming us.

Now all becomes clear concerning the restoration of the dominion of man over creation. He lost it, he was unable to regain it, but through the Lord Jesus who identified Himself with us, took our debt of sin upon Himself, paid the full penalty of death for us, met every condition of God's holy law, He once again lays claim for us to the original purpose of God for man, as stated in Genesis:

> . . . and have dominion over the fish of the sea, and over the fowl of the air, and over every living thing that moveth upon the earth (Gen. 1:28).

But the full realization of this must wait until He comes again to set up His kingdom on this earth as the Second Man, the Last Adam, the Man from heaven. You see then, there is much more to salvation than just being saved from hell, and going to heaven when we die. When we receive Jesus Christ as Saviour these two things are settled forever, but after that, our position, our place and authority in the coming Kingdom will be determined on how we have lived and served Him after we were saved. Before the setting up of the Kingdom and the restoration of creation there will be a Judgment Seat of Christ, where the various places in the Kingdom will be assigned to believers on the basis of their works. Some will reign over five cities, some over ten, others will lose all reward and be "saved so as by fire." Failure to heed God's admonition to live a life of growth in grace, separation from the world, and a complete dedication to His service, will result in "suffering loss," and some will be "ashamed . . . at his coming" (I John 2:28). Some will fall short of a full reward (II John 8). Others will have an abundant entrance (II Pet. 1:11).

The motive for service and a yielded, fruitful walk must, therefore, be on the basis of what Jesus did for us at Calvary. Only as we realize fully His identification with our sins, and our identification with His death and resurrection shall we be able to serve Him acceptably. It must be first of all a service of gratitude for including us in the grace of redemption. What happened to Christ is imputed to us. We are now one with Him. The author of Hebrews says:

> For both he that sanctifieth and they who are sanctified are all of one: for which cause he is not ashamed to call them brethren,
> Saying, I will declare thy name unto my brethren, in the midst of the church [congregation] will I sing praise unto thee.
> And again, I will put my trust in him. And again, Behold I and the children which God hath given me (Heb. 2:11-13).

JESUS NOT ASHAMED

Of all the precious lessons in these verses, there is one prominent, outstanding revelation. Jesus the Son of God, Creator of the worlds, was *not ashamed* to identify Himself with miserable, unworthy, helpless, hopeless, filthy sinners, but was willing to die for all such. He endured the Cross and despised the shame. He now calls us "brethren." And can it be that we, lifted from the mire and slime of sin should be ashamed of Him, the Altogether Lovely One? How inconsistent for anyone washed in the blood to be ashamed of His Name! How ungrateful to be anything less than our best for Him! How awful to withhold anything of all we are and have from Him! It seems to me that once we realize what He did for us, we would never be satisfied until everything was on the altar for Him.

The balance of Hebrews two enforces this argument and leaves no excuse for anyone to live on a low plane of Christian conduct.

> Forasmuch then as the children are partakers of flesh and blood, he also himself likewise took part of the same; that through death he might destroy him that had the power of death, that is, the devil;
> And deliver them who through fear of death were all their lifetime subject to bondage (Heb. 2:14, 15).

How far have you progressed in this path of surrender? Or have you "neglected" this great salvation? Will you today yield your all to Him, deny all self-will, separate from all evil and receive the joy of victorious living? If you fear it will cost too much and you cannot hold out, then we point you to the closing verse of our chapter:

> Wherefore in all things it behoved him to be made like unto his brethren, that he might be a merciful and faithful high priest in things pertaining to God, to make reconciliation for the sins of the people.
> For in that he himself hath suffered being tempted, he is able to succour them that are tempted (Heb. 2:17, 18).

Christ is already the Victor. Satan is already a defeated foe, and we need not fear his onslaughts as long as we follow our victorious Captain. The war ended at the empty tomb and all that remains of the enemy is the "mopping up," till he shall be cast into the lake of fire.

Look up to Him for help, look ahead to the reward for your

encouragement. In view of the infinite price of your redemption, do you dare to yield your all to Him, and trust Him to see you through? Judge and confess everything of self and the flesh, and appropriate the promise:

> If a man therefore purge himself from these, he shall be a vessel unto honour, sanctified, and meet for the master's use, and prepared unto every good work (II Tim. 2:21).

CHAPTER FIVE

All Out—but Not All In

> Wherefore, holy brethren, partakers of the heavenly calling, consider the Apostle and High Priest of our profession, Christ Jesus;
>
> Who was faithful to him that appointed him, as also Moses was faithful in all his house (Heb. 3:1, 2).

AN indispensable rule in the correct interpretation of any passage of Scripture is to determine first to whom the passage is addressed. To apply what God has to say about believers to sinners will distort the entire meaning, and lead to confusion. Just one pertinent example will make clear what we mean. In Matthew 11:29 Jesus said:

> Take my yoke upon you, and learn of me; for I am meek and lowly in heart: and ye shall find rest unto your souls.

To apply this to the sinner for salvation will contradict the entire revelation of all other Scriptures which declare salvation as the free gift of God. The sinner is not saved by taking a yoke upon him. A yoke is the symbol of work, labor and toil. The sinner is not saved by working and carrying a yoke or bearing a cross. He is saved by faith in Christ. Paul tells us:

> But to him that worketh not, but believeth . . . his faith is counted for righteousness (Rom. 4:5).

Taking the yoke of Matthew 11:29 is God's invitation to *saints*. The invitation to sinners is in the previous verse:

> Come unto me, all ye that labour and are heavy laden, and I will give you rest (Matt. 11:28).

48

This is salvation for those who had been laboring and were heavy laden and struggling under their futile efforts to save themselves. These can find rest only by ceasing from their own labors, and just coming to Christ for salvation. But this is not the end, for something follows. To those who have come to Christ for salvation, He now says, "I want you to go further and go on to the 'abundant life' of victory in service." You are saved by grace, but victory comes only by sacrifice. So now go on. Take the next step: "Take my yoke upon you, and learn of me."

Now that you are saved, get busy and go to work, and you will find an additional rest and peace, over and above the "rest" of salvation. The "Come unto me" of Matthew 11:28 is for sinners; the "Take my yoke upon you" is for saints who have already come to Christ for the "rest" of salvation. Failure to distinguish to whom the Scripture is addressed results in confusion, and as a result we have preachers urging people to work, give up things, sell all they have to give to the poor, as conditions of salvation, which is a denial of salvation by grace. Salvation for the sinner is by doing nothing but receiving the grace of God. And then works and progress must follow. How much of preaching is an unholy union of grace and works!

DON'T NEGLECT SALVATION

This rule must be applied in our study of Hebrews or we will be confused and find the Bible contradicting itself. We make no apology for repeating that the Book of Hebrews is addressed to believers, born-again, saved believers who had taken the first step of Matthew 11:28, but then had halted short of the life of victory and surrender of Matthew 11:29. They had remained babes who still needed milk. They were like their forefathers, out of Egypt forever, but never reaching the land of victory; instead they were dying in the wilderness. They had "neglected" their salvation (Heb. 2:3); they had let their duties and responsibilities slip, and had "come short" of God's best for their lives (Heb. 4:1).

Holy Brethren

To begin the study of Hebrews with the traditional preconceived idea that it was written to religious, unconverted professors who came short of salvation, is to be in a dense fog all
the rest of the way, facing irreconcilable obstacles. These people
addressed did not come short of salvation, but were in danger
of coming short of a life of service and victory and rewards at
the Judgment Seat of Christ. This is evident from the various
ways in which they are addressed. And so Hebrews three opens
as follows:

> Wherefore, holy brethren, partakers of the heavenly calling . . . .

The opening word "wherefore" connects this verse with the
preceding one. Because of what Jesus was and did and is, they
are admonished to keep their eyes on Him, and Him alone, for
victory. Notice they are called "holy brethren." They were by
no means sinlessly perfect in their walk, for then there would
be no need or occasion to urge them to go on to perfection.
They were "holy" in their standing in Christ through faith.
Positionally they were holy, sanctified and separated unto God
but in their walk they still came far short. But they *were*
brethren just the same, and partakers of the heavenly calling.
They were saved by the faith *of* Christ and are now urged to be
faithful *to* Christ. The word translated "partakers" indicates
the closest kind of relationship. It means to share, to be of the
same substance. It is the same word translated "fellows" in
Hebrews 1:9. Peter says we are "partakers of Christ's sufferings" (I Pet. 4:13). Again he says we are "partakers of the
divine nature" (II Pet. 1:4). Paul says that God "hath made us
meet to be partakers of the inheritance of the saints in light"
(Col. 1:12). Or consider Paul's words in I Corinthians 10:17:

> For we being many are one bread and one body: for we are all
> partakers of that one bread.

When these Hebrews, therefore, are addressed as "holy
brethren, partakers of the heavenly calling," it indicates oneness

with Christ, the most intimate and inseparable union as members of one body. What right have we then to say that the persons addressed in Hebrews were unconverted professors who had gone along with the Gospel, but fell short of being actually saved? We stress this point, for to make these Hebrews anything but born-again believers is to violate the simplest rules of grammar.

CONSIDER HIM

Furthermore, they are admonished to "consider the Apostle and High Priest of our profession, Christ Jesus." Jesus is not the sinner's High Priest. Until the sinner has received Him as Saviour he cannot be anything else but his Judge — not his Intercessor. All that Christ could do for the sinner was done at Calvary, and until the sinner stops first at the Cross, He has no access to the Priest. Our Lord in heaven is powerless to do anything for the sinner until he comes first by the way of the Cross of Calvary. That is why Jesus in heaven does not pray for sinners today. His priestly work at the right hand of God is exclusively for saints. He did all He could do for sinners when He died for them, and until they come to Him as their substitute and Saviour, He cannot intercede or pray for them. He Himself said:

> I pray for them [believers]: I pray not for the world, but for them which thou hast given me; for they are thine (John 17:9).

He prays for His own that they may be sanctified and become fruitful. Because of His faithfulness to us, we are admonished to be faithful in our Christian service and walk. The faithfulness of Christ should be our motive for our faithfulness to Him,

> Who was faithful to him that appointed him, as also Moses was faithful in all his house (Heb. 3:2).

An illustration is now introduced, and Moses is taken as an example. Moses is said to have been faithful in all his house. It is not said that he was perfect, that he never made a mistake,

that he was sinless, but *he was faithful.* This faithfulness was
as a "servant" of God. He was faithful,

> . . . for a testimony of those things which were to be spoken
> after (Heb. 3:5).

While Christ is compared to Moses, this comparison is designed to show the superiority of the faithfulness of Christ over
that of Moses. It is pinpointed by the use of two little words.
Christ was faithful "as a Son *over* his own house [the house of
God]" (Heb. 3:6). "Moses was faithful *in* all his house," as
a servant. These Hebrew Christians revered and honored Moses,
and were sorely tempted to put themselves back under the law
of Moses, and therefore are reminded of the infinite superiority
of Christ over Moses and of grace over the law. Moses, far
from being perfect, was faithful in his testimony concerning
the revelation of God. What he was told to write he faithfully
performed. What he said could be depended upon by all in his
house. So too (but in a much greater sense) we can trust the
Word of Christ and rest securely upon His promises, for the
same message which Moses wrote was fulfilled in the coming of
the greater One than Moses.

The expression at the close of verse six has given trouble
for many, in view of our salvation by grace.

> But Christ as a son over his own house; whose house are we,
> if we hold fast the confidence and the rejoicing of the hope firm
> unto the end (Heb. 3:6).

On the surface it seems that this verse indicates that the believer can ultimately be lost, for being the house of God is made
dependent upon holding fast. However, this passage is not
dealing with salvation, but with assurance, confidence and rejoicing in hope. The danger was not that these believers could
lose their salvation, but they could lose their assurance, their
confidence, their joy, and finally the reward for faithfulness. It
is not "if we hold fast our *salvation,*" but if we "hold fast our
confidence." And this is in perfect harmony with the central
theme of the epistle. These Hebrew Christians were hated and

despised, looked upon as the refuse and offscouring of society, and were gravely tempted to go back to the easier path of compromise. If they surrendered their separated position and cut the corners and toned down their testimony, it might save them persecution and criticism. But in doing so they would lose their confidence, hope and assurance. They would put a stop to their growth in grace and like the Galatians slip back into legalism and remain in spiritual infancy. Instead of fainting under the testings and trials resulting from our faithfulness, we need to heed the words of Peter:

> Beloved, think it not strange concerning the fiery trial which is to try you, as though some strange thing happened unto you:
> But rejoice, inasmuch as ye are partakers of Christ's sufferings; that, when his glory shall be revealed, ye may be glad also with exceeding joy (I Pet. 4:12, 13).

Look ahead to the glory and up to Jesus, and you will not go down in defeat. Christ's faithfulness in saving us cost Him His life, and our faithfulness to Him also means paying the price. Remember, therefore, our salvation depends upon His faithfulness, but our rewards are dependent upon *our* faithfulness in holding fast our confidence, and rejoicing in hope firm unto the end. Only an out-an-out Christian can have the full assurance and joy of salvation. There is no greater joy than to know one is in the will of the Lord, doing what pleases Him, and serving in the place where He wants one. It may not be an easy place, it may cost a great deal, but in the midst of it all is a deep, undisturbed peace in knowing, "I am where God wants me, and doing what He wishes me to do."

Have You Lost Something?

Have you lost that joy which once you knew? Have the temptations of life overcome you, and do you sometimes wonder if your salvation is real? Are you discouraged because of the little progress you are able to see in your life? Then let me give you the remedy, if sometimes you feel the price of faithfulness is too great.

1. First look back to Calvary and consider once again at what an awful cost you were redeemed. Look back at your life before you received Christ, when you were condemned, lost and on the way to an eternal hell. See what it cost Him to redeem you.

2. Now look up and see this same Jesus at the right hand of God, interceding for you, and offering you forgiveness for your neglect and failure, and assuring you that there is all-sufficient grace for every trial and test and temptation.

3. Look ahead and behold the same Jesus, waiting for the crowning day when He will return to reward His servants on the basis of faithfulness. Get your eyes off things and men and self, and

> . . . consider him that endured such contradiction of sinners against himself, lest ye be wearied and faint in your minds (Heb. 12:3).

It is all a matter of perspective. It depends on whether you consider only the present, or have your eyes on the future. If only we can translate our present suffering and sacrifice for Christ into terms of eternity's reward, we will be ashamed that we ever murmured or complained. If only we interpret the trials of the way in the light of the glory at the end of the road, all our troubles will melt away and with Paul we can say:

> For I reckon that the sufferings of this present time are not worthy to be compared with the glory which shall be revealed in us (Rom. 8:18).

> Oft times the day seems long,
>   Our trials hard to bear;
> We're tempted to complain,
>   To murmur and despair;
> But Christ will soon appear,
>   To catch His Bride away,
> All tears forever over,
>   In God's eternal day.

> It will be worth it all,
>   When we see Jesus;
> Life's trials will seem so small,
>   When we see Christ;

> One glimpse of His dear face,
> All sorrow will erase,
> So gladly run the race,
> Till we see Christ.

Cast not away therefore your confidence, which hath great recompence of reward.

For ye have need of patience, that, after ye have done the will of God, ye might receive the promise [reward].

For yet a little while, and he that shall come will come, and will not tarry (Heb. 10:35-37).

CHAPTER SIX

Carcasses in the Wilderness

THE Christian life begins with a new birth from above. We are said to be born of God and as such are children of God the moment we are saved. As in the natural, so in the spiritual — We are born "infants." But we are not to remain "babes" forever, we are to grow up and develop into mature, spiritual manhood. However, sad though it be, many of God's children seem to be stunted and suffering from arrested development. They are children in the family of God, but make little progress — remaining perpetual infants. In most cases it is a feeding problem, failure to feed upon the sincere milk of the Word. We would say it kindly yet firmly, that the average believer knows tragically little about the Bible. Ignorance of the Scriptures is appalling among many Christians who have been saved for years. As a result they are weak and anemic and fall easy prey to temptation, false doctrine and error, in both faith and practice. This was the situation among the Hebrew Christians to whom the Book of Hebrews was addressed. They had stopped short in their spiritual development and growth, and whereas they should have been teachers, they had need that they be taught again the very ABC's of the oracles of God, and were able to take only milk, baby food, and not solid food (Heb. 5:12).

The cause lay in the fact that they had neglected the Word of this great salvation (Heb. 2:3) first spoken by the Lord, and then recorded by them that heard Him (Heb. 1:1). It is safe to say that all those who stumble and creep along in their perpetual infancy and underdevelopment do so from one primary cause — neglect of Bible study. You tell me how much time you spend with your Bible, and I will accurately mark your report card of Christian progress. It was to correct this neglect that Hebrews was written. The message is: Go on, go on till the crown is won, go on to maturity. Neglect to do so will not go unpunished. Failure to obey Christ will result in the chastening of the Lord, and loss of reward at the end of the journey.

THE CASE OF ISRAEL

In illustrating the danger of stopping short of God's best, the author of Hebrews now introduces the history of the children of Israel. This would be familiar ground for these Hebrew Christians who were fully acquainted with their nation's history, as recorded in the Old Testament. So they are pointed to the experience of the nation, as a warning against halting short of the abundant life.

> Wherefore (as the Holy Ghost saith, To day if ye will hear his voice,
> Harden not your hearts, as in the provocation, in the day of temptation in the wilderness:
> When your fathers tempted me, proved me, and saw my works forty years.
> Wherefore I was grieved with that generation, and said, They do always err in their heart; and they have not known my ways.
> So I sware in my wrath, They shall not enter into my rest) (Heb. 3:7-11).

All of this section, except the first word "Wherefore," is a parenthesis, to serve as a warning in view of what had preceded it. The quotation is from the ninety-fifth Psalm. In this psalm the writer exhorts the people of God to yield Him full obedience. He says:

> O come, let us worship and bow down; let us kneel before the LORD our Maker.
> For he is our God; and we are the people of his pasture, and the sheep of his hand (Ps. 95:6, 7).

The message is to God's people, saved and redeemed and delivered, and because of this they are warned in the words quoted in Hebrews three,

> . . . To day if ye will hear his voice, Harden not your hearts (Heb. 3:7, 8).

Hardened Christians

It is evidently possible, yea, it is an ever-present danger, that believers, born-again children of God, can harden their hearts against God. We talk about hardened sinners, but here we have hardened saints. Living in disobedience to God's will, continuing to ignore God's warnings and pleadings, results in a benumbing of their sensitivity toward Him, and they become callous to His tender pleadings until at last it brings them to a place where "it is impossible to renew them again to repentance" and God can only deal with them in chastening and judgment at the Judgment Seat of Christ where it will be burned out, and they shall be saved, yet so as by fire.

Do you remember how convicted you were when, after you were saved, you were faced with the need of giving up some sin or habit? You knew that thing had no place in your new-found life, and you were miserable in your defeat and disobedience? But as time went on, the conviction seemed to become stifled, you began to find excuses, and today the very thing which once caused you such a feeling of guilt and conviction is condoned and excused without a twinge of conscience. Do you know what has happened? You have hardened your heart, and right there is the reason why you have not grown spiritually, and you know nothing of victory. Yes, yes, I believe you are saved, but you are losing out terribly in forfeited blessing and reward.

Witness the case of Israel. They had been enslaved in Egypt under the cruel whip of their taskmasters. By sovereign grace God had delivered them by blood and by power. He had saved them from their miserable bondage and slavery. They were under the blood, a redeemed people *out* of Egypt, never to return again. But that was only the beginning of the journey – Canaan was the goal. God not only wanted them *out* of Egypt, but *in* the land of Canaan. Between these lay a wilderness journey which seemed indeed impassable. But God made provision for their safe arrival in Canaan *if* they would obey Him and trust Him. He put the Red Sea between them and Egypt so they could not go back. He provided a pillar of cloud and of fire to inerrantly guide them. He gave them manna from heaven and water from the rock. Their clothes never became threadbare and their shoes did not wear out. What an adequate provision was theirs with every need supplied!

SHORT OF CANAAN

Yet only two Israelites over twenty years of age who left Egypt ever reached Canaan. The rest of them, dissatisfied with God's provision, lusted for the old diet, and while they were out of Egypt, they still had the old Egypt in them. They yielded to their carnal appetites and desired the fish and the leeks, onions, garlic, melons and cucumbers of Egypt and despised God's heaven-sent manna. Now remember, these were God's people, redeemed by the blood, delivered from slavery out of Egypt, never to return. But of them God says:

> Wherefore I was grieved with that generation . . . .
> So I sware in my wrath, They shall not enter into my rest (Heb. 3:10, 11).

What rest is meant here by the Lord? Was it the "rest" of redemption? It could not be that, for they already had received that "rest" by being delivered from the brick kilns of Egypt. It was the "rest" of the land of Canaan, the land of victory and the abundant life of milk and honey, corn and wine. God did not send them back into Egypt when they sinned to "unredeem" them again. They were still redeemed from Egypt, but fell short of Canaan and died in the wilderness. Dying in the wilderness! What a tragic fate for a redeemed people!

The sin which prevented them from entering Canaan was

disobedience to God, failure to trust and obey Him. It was unbelief on the part of a redeemed people.

> And to whom sware he that they should not enter into his rest,
> but to them that believed not?
> So we see that they could not enter in because of unbelief
> (Heb. 3:18, 19).

What was the thing which they would not believe? It was
the report of the spies, Caleb and Joshua, and their counsel to
go up immediately to take the land and possess it. They were
at the very borders of the promised land when the twelve spies
were sent out. When they returned with their report of great
walled cities and men of giant stature, they failed to reckon with
God, and as a result turned back into the wilderness for thirty-
eight more years, to perish in the desert after having been at
the very threshold of victory.

For Our Admonition

Now all these things were recorded for our admonition and
warning. Israel is a picture of the believer. Egypt is a type of
the world of sin and bondage in which we as sinners were enslaved. Moses, their deliverer, was a type of Christ. The Passover Lamb was a picture of Christ, and the blood of the lamb of
redemption pointed to the blood of Christ. The drowning of
Pharaoh's host in the Red Sea speaks of our security forever
in Christ. The pillar of cloud is the guiding Holy Spirit. The
manna was Christ, the Bread of Life, and the water from the
rock speaks of the Word of God, the Bible, as the Rock was
Christ the living Word. Canaan is God's picture of the life of
victory. Canaan is *not* a picture of heaven. Canaan represents
the abundant victorious life of the believer here and now.
Canaan cannot represent heaven, for Canaan had to be possessed
by conquest. Canaan was a land of fighting, and Israel must
battle fiercely to possess it, gaining the victory but also even
suffering temporary defeat. Canaan cannot be heaven, for in
heaven, thank God, we shall not have to fight to get the vic-

tory. The Israelites were completely out of Egypt, but came short of reaching the land of the abundant life, the Canaan of victory.

This is the teaching of the parenthesis of Hebrews three, in verses seven to eleven, and now we take up the application:

> Take heed, brethren, lest there be in any of you an evil heart of unbelief, in departing from the living God.
>
> But exhort one another daily, while it is called To day; lest any of you be hardened through the deceitfulness of sin (Heb. 3: 12, 13).

That is what we are trying to do in these messages, to warn you and exhort you not to make Israel's mistake, but to become partakers of the full blessing and victory which God has in store for every believer who will be obedient to His will.

It is possible for believers, here called "brethren, partakers of the heavenly calling," to depart from the living God through neglect and disobedience, being saved but defeated, failing God and never reaching spiritual maturity and victory. Salvation is the free gift of God, but to become "partakers of the *reward*" means holding "the beginning of our confidence stedfast unto the end." It is in no sense a matter of salvation, but a question of communion and fellowship. By faith our standing in Christ is assured once for all, but there is more than just standing. Some Christians are so satisfied with their standing, security and position in grace that they do nothing else but "stand." They have stood for years just where they started. But to make progress means to walk. Our union with Christ assures our standing; our communion depends upon our walking.

> If we walk in the light, as he is in the light, we have fellowship one with another, and the blood of Jesus Christ his Son cleanseth us from all sin (I John 1:7).

How far, Christian friend, have you walked since the day of your conversion? Some of you have been saved for twenty, thirty, forty years and are no nearer to Canaan and victory than you were then. Make the test for yourself. Ask yourself, Have

I the joy I first knew at the beginning? Do I love the study of God's Word more today than a year ago? Do I pray as much as I used to, and have I had any recent answers to prayer? Do I witness as I did when I was in my first love? If your honest answer must be "No, I can see little progress in my Christian life," then you cannot come to the place of victory, and the possession of the abundant life. Have you become cold, critical, cynical and sour, instead of mellowing and sweetening with the passage of the years of your Christian experience? Then you are wandering in the wilderness and will come to the end without ever knowing the full peace of God, and will stand ashamed and empty-handed before Him in that day.

Only Eleven Days

The illustration of Israel whose carcasses fell in the wilderness leaves no excuse for us to repeat their experience. Moses had led Israel out of Egypt and brought them to the very edge of Canaan at Kadesh-barnea, and then, because they were afraid of the battle for Canaan, turned back, way back to Horeb. And then God says:

> (There are eleven days' journey from Horeb . . . unto Kadesh-barnea) (Deut. 1:2).

Only eleven days journey from Horeb to the very gateway of the promised land, Kadesh-barnea. Here God spoke to them by Moses:

> . . . Ye have dwelt long enough in this mount:
> Turn you, and take your journey . . . .
> Behold, I have set the land before you: go in and possess the land which the LORD sware unto your fathers (Deut. 1:6-8).

And yet, instead of obeying God to go forward and possess their inheritance they rebelled and wandered for another thirty-eight years in the wilderness of defeat. It took them forty years to make a journey of only eleven days, and their carcasses fell in the wilderness.

The next chapter, Hebrews four, begins with a personal application which we take up in our next message, but we want to close this lesson with its warning.

> Let us therefore fear, lest, a promise being left us of entering into his rest, any of you should seem to come short of it (Heb. 4:1).

Oh, believer, in the light of the Judgment Seat of Christ, will you arise, turn about, and leaving behind all doubt and disobedience, claim the land of victory and find a rest and peace you never knew before? The way is clear; honestly judge everything in your life which cannot bear the examination of your Saviour, confess it and forsake it.

CHAPTER SEVEN

The Rest of Labor

IT is possible for a person to be saved and destined for heaven, yet lead a miserable, defeated life here below. The Bible is perfectly clear that there are two distinct possibilities of Christian experience: defeat or victory. Paul recognizes this fact and speaks of carnal believers and spiritual believers; perpetual babes in Christ never growing up, and mature, grown-up spiritual men. The burden of the Book of Hebrews is to induce the Hebrew Christians addressed to grow into maturity and not remain spiritual infants by failing to obey the Lord. His plea is summed up in the words:

> For when for the time ye ought to be teachers, ye have need that one teach you again which be the first principles of the oracles of God; and are become such as have need of milk [baby food], and not of strong meat [solid food] (Heb. 5:12).

The tragedy is that many believers are perpetual infants, suffering from undernourishment and arrested development and malnutrition, lacking joy and victory and reward. It is no use denying the fact that too many believers are no farther along today than they were five years ago. This is not God's will, for He has something better. It is possible to know an undisturbed rest and peace, an attainment of victory over self and the world, which passeth all understanding. Why then go on defeated and discouraged, when the fullness of the abundant life can be yours? We trust these studies in Hebrews will show you the way. Jesus said:

> These things have I spoken unto you, that my joy might remain in you, and that your joy might be full (John 15:11).

Again He says in John 16:24:

> . . . ask, and ye shall receive, that your joy may be full.

It is then possible to be saved and never come to the fullness of the joy of our salvation here below. As a striking example of, and solemn warning against this tragedy, the author of Hebrews calls our attention to the experience of Israel, quoting from the ninety-fifth Psalm. Israel was a redeemed people, delivered by God from Egypt. It was all of grace, by the death of a lamb and the shedding of the blood. They were now out of Egypt, but their goal was Canaan and victory. They were delivered from the slavery of Egypt, but had not yet conquered the giants of Canaan. Between the two lay a wilderness which could have been crossed in eleven days, but instead it took them forty years, and the great mass of them died before ever seeing victory in Canaan. Out of Egypt but never knowing the fullness of the joy of victory in Canaan!

A Solemn Warning

This example of unbelief and disobedience is given as a solemn warning to Christians. It is addressed to believers, redeemed by the blood but still floundering about in the desert of disobedience and unwillingness to follow Christ all the way. And so Hebrews four opens with the admonition:

> Let us therefore fear, lest, a promise being left us of entering into his rest, any of you should seem to come short of it (Heb. 4:1).

The prominent word in this chapter is REST. It is the subject of this entire section, and occurs no less than eleven times from Hebrews 3:11 to Hebrews 4:11. There are three kinds of rest mentioned: a past rest, a present rest and a future rest. The past rest is the rest of salvation; the present rest is the rest of victory over sin; and the future rest is the eternal rest in heaven when all our labors and trials will be over. All these three *rests* are mentioned in the passage, but it is one special rest we are considering, and the other two are introduced only for clarification. There is a rest which is the result of receiving Christ by faith, another rest which comes only as we walk obediently according to His Word, and a future rest which awaits all God's people after this life is over. The first and the third rest are God's past gift and future promise. They do not depend on our works, but upon *His* work, and so cannot be lost. But the second "rest," the rest of service and the peace of victory, is a present possibility and depends upon *our* labors, and our faithfulness; and because it depends upon our faithfulness it can be lost, and hence the warning, "lest any of you should seem to come short of it."

In verses nine to eleven of Hebrews four these three "rests" are clearly defined. In Hebrews 4:9 we have the future rest which awaits all God's children: "There remaineth therefore a rest to the people of God." This is the eternal rest of which John says:

> . . . Blessed are the dead which die in the Lord from henceforth: Yea, saith the Spirit, that they may rest from their labours; and their works do follow them (Rev. 14:13).

This is the portion of every believer. But in the very next verse of Hebrews four it speaks of quite another rest, one which is already an accomplished fact:

> For he that is entered into his rest, he also hath ceased from his own works, as God did from his (Heb. 4:10).

This is a past rest and is the rest of salvation. It is the rest of Matthew 11:28, "Come unto me, all ye that labour and are heavy laden, and I will give you rest." It is a given rest, not one which is earned by labor and works. It is a rest which comes only to those who *stop* their own works, and disowning all merit or righteousness of their own, come as poor, helpless, exhausted sinners to the Lamb of God for salvation. For this rest we do not work or strive, we cannot purchase it or deserve it. It is only for

> . . . him that worketh not, but believeth on him that justifieth the ungodly, his faith is counted for righteousness (Rom. 4:5).

Works are entirely excluded. But now notice the strange contrast presented in the very next verse of Hebrews four. After stating that "rest" comes only to those who *stop* working for it, this verse continues:

> Let us labour therefore to enter into that rest, lest any man fall after the same example of unbelief [the example of Israel] (Heb. 4:11).

Here is a rest which comes only by labor and sacrifice, by toiling and working. Let us labor for this rest. There is a rest which every believer possesses the moment he receives Christ. There is another rest which comes only to those who will follow Him in the path of obedience and service. These two possibilities of Christian experience are abundantly illustrated in the Scriptures. Jesus mentions a "life," and a life "more abundantly" (John 10:10). Paul mentions two kinds of peace; a peace *with* God which every believer already *has,* and a peace *of* God which is only for those who yield and surrender to His will. The peace with God is the gift of God.

> Therefore being justified by faith we have peace with God through our Lord Jesus Christ (Rom. 5:1).

This peace we *have* as a result of coming to Christ in faith. But there is another peace mentioned in Philippians 4:6,7:

> Be careful for nothing; but in everything by prayer and supplication with thanksgiving let your requests be made known unto God.
>
> And the peace of God, which passeth all understanding, shall keep your hearts and minds through Christ Jesus.

This peace *of* God is conditional and comes when we turn everything over to God, without reservation, "by prayer and thanksgiving, let [our] requests be made known," tell Him all about it, surrender the battle into His hands, and go on to victory. Thousands who are at peace *with* God never know the

"peace of God" which comes by a full surrender to Christ.
These are two distinct possibilities of Christian experience.
They are clearly given by Jesus in Matthew 11:28, 29:

> Come unto me, all ye that labour and are heavy laden, and
> I will give you rest.
> Take my yoke upon you, and learn of me; for I am meek and
> lowly in heart: and ye shall find rest unto your souls.

As we have pointed out before, this is not one and the same
invitation, but two distinct calls. The first word in verse twenty-
eight is *come*, while the first word in verse twenty-nine is *take*.
The invitation to come is for the sinner. It is to them who labor
in vain and are heavy laden. To those who thus come to Christ,
having nothing to offer or to bring, He gives rest. It is a gift; it
is free; it costs the sinner nothing; it is all of grace. This is
the "rest" of salvation and peace *with* God. It is obtained by
coming *to* Christ.

The next verse, however, is quite a different thing. It is now
addressed to those who have already come and received the
free gift. But He does not want the believer to stop with this
rest, for there is more. And so to those who have come and are
saved, He says now: "Take my yoke upon you."

The believer who already has salvation without working for
it, is now invited to take something and go to work for Him.
A yoke is the symbol of subjection, obedience, labor and service.
We are forever free from the yoke of sin and the law which
was hard and cruel, and in gratitude for this deliverance we
now are to take His yoke which is easy because He carries the
heavy end. The result of carrying His yoke, subjecting yourself
to His will, surrendering all and yielding your whole life to
Him is "rest for your souls." This is not the rest of verse twenty-
eight. That rest is "given" to us. Jesus says, "I will give you
rest." But this other rest by carrying the yoke must be worked
for and be diligently sought, for we read, "ye shall *find* rest
unto your souls."

In the great congregation of Israel which was delivered from the yoke of Egypt, there were but a few who were willing to take that yoke of obedience and surrender to go, and these alone were permitted to enter Canaan and find the "second rest." The others all perished in the wilderness. To every believer comes this call. We have already come *to* Jesus for salvation, but now comes the call to service, to a dedicated life of obedience and trust. The second call is just as definite as the first, and requires just as definite a decision. After we are saved, we have the choice of going on to victory in Canaan, or dying in the wilderness of defeat.

It was so with Israel. Soon after their deliverance from Egypt, God brought them to the very borders of Canaan at Kadesh-barnea and placed before them a definite choice. They had received the report of the spies and God now faces them with an important decision. The command was clear. Moses said to them at the very portal of victory:

> Behold, the LORD thy God hath set the land before thee: go and possess it, as the LORD God of thy fathers hath said unto thee; fear not, neither be discouraged.
> Notwithstanding ye would not go up, but rebelled against the commandment of the LORD your God:
> And ye murmured in your tents . . . .
> The people is greater and taller than we; the cities are great and walled up to heaven; and moreover we have seen the sons of the Anakims [giants] there.
> Then I said unto you, Dread not, neither be afraid of them.
> The LORD your God which goeth before you he shall fight for you, according to all that he did for you in Egypt before your eyes (Deut. 1:21, 26-30).

The decision was clearly up to them. Would they obey God, trust Him fully, or listen to the flesh? It was a momentous occasion, for much depended upon it. They made the wrong decision and the sad record continues:

> Yet in this thing ye did not believe the LORD your God (Deut. 1:32).

They hardened their hearts and instead of victory with God, they went down in defeat to the flesh. Listen to the result:

> And the LORD heard the voice of your words, and was wroth, and sware, saying,
> Surely there shall not one of these men of this evil generation see the good land (Deut. 1:34, 35).

This is the incident to which Hebrews three and four refer us, and we are warned not to make the same mistake. Many of you are standing where Israel stood at Kadesh-barnea. You too are saved, but defeated because of disobedience, your lack of separation from the world, because of neglect of God's Word, because of weights of this world, unconfessed sins, and fear of paying the price of an all-out yielding to Christ. He is calling to you to dedicate your all to Him and trust Him completely, and you too are hesitating, for the price of full surrender seems great.

But God only uses those who are willing to obey. Every great servant of God of whom I have ever known had these two experiences: First they came as lost sinners to Christ for salvation; then sooner or later they were faced with God's call to complete obedience in yielding their lives for service to Christ. Call it dedication, consecration, full surrender, second blessing, complete yielding or what you will, it is the crying need of this day. Too many think of the Christian life as merely escaping hell and going to heaven, but know nothing of the joy of service and life of complete surrender, and the peace of God here and now, and a glorious reward by and by.

Carefully weigh the question. Will it be victory in Canaan, or wandering in the wilderness of regrets for not daring to follow Jesus all the way? Examine your heart today, look at what your redemption cost Him, and ask yourself, "Can I withhold aught from Him who gave His all for me?" Don't you hear His call now? "Follow me, and I will make you to become fishers of men." Follow Me! He will go before you, if you dare to trust Him, and if you dare turn your life, which has been so drab and fruitless, over to Him to do as He pleases. Stop choosing your own path, let Him lead and it will bring you to victory! *Victory!*

> It may not be on the mountain's height,
>   Or over the stormy sea;
> It may not be at the battle's front
>   My Lord will have need of me;
> But if by a still, small voice He calls
>   To paths that I do not know,
> I'll answer, dear Lord, with my hand in Thine,
>   I'll go where you want me to go.
>
> I'll go where you want me to go, dear Lord,
>   O'er mountain, or plain, or sea;
> I'll say what you want me to say, dear Lord,
>   I'll be what you want me to be.

CHAPTER EIGHT

The Second Blessing

> Let us therefore fear, lest, a promise being left us of entering into his rest, any of you should seem to come short of it.
>
> For unto us was the gospel preached, as well as unto them [Israel]: but the word preached did not profit them, not being mixed with faith in them that heard it.
>
> For we which have believed do enter into rest, as he said, As I have sworn in my wrath, if they shall enter into my rest: although the works were finished from the foundation of the world (Heb. 4:1-3).

GOD has many blessings for His people, and since there are so many, there must of necessity be a first and a second blessing. These two are clearly defined in the Scriptures. The first is the blessing of salvation; the second is the blessing of victory and obedient service to Him who hath saved us. The first blessing of salvation all believers share alike, but the second blessing is reserved only for those who will pay the price. It is a sad fact, that many sincere but mistaken believers have corrupted and distorted the meaning of the "second blessing" and attribute it to all sorts of unscriptural methods, feelings and emotions. It is not a baptism in the Spirit or a second definite work of salvation. It is instead a definite blessing which comes when the believer solemnly faces the claims of Christ upon his life, and determines by God's grace to forsake everything which is displeasing to God. It may be accompanied by deep emotions and feelings, or it may come without the shedding of a tear. It may come in response to a powerful sermon on dedication, or may take place in the quietness of one's room as one seeks

God's will by prayer and searching the Scriptures. It may come at the time of conversion or a long time after, but it is a definite experience accompanied by definite results and blessings. There are many blessings, a third, a fourth, and so on, which are just as definite, whenever a believer, as he grows in grace and receives new light on the Word, yields something to God in obedience to His will. Because of the abuse of the term "second blessing," it were better to drop the expression entirely and refer to it in Scriptural terms as: yielding, obedience, forsaking self, and following Christ.

ISRAEL'S EXPERIENCE

In the Book of Hebrews, the writer in pleading with these Hebrew Christians to go on to this blessing of victory, reminds them of Israel's experience. They were saved from Egypt when they believed God's command concerning the blood. Later they were challenged by a second command, "Go up, and possess the land." They were faced with a decision — "Go on," or "Go back." This promise they neglected, and chose the life of ease in the wilderness rather than the battles of Canaan. Going into Canaan meant work, sacrifice and great battles. In the wilderness they had nothing to do but loll and laze and loaf about, under the provision of God's great social security program. All their needs were supplied. Their food fell from heaven to be merely gathered. They did not have to plow or hoe or harvest. Their drink gushed out before them from the rock. They did not have to dig wells or build pumps for their water. They did not have to mend their clothes or repair their shoes, for they did not wear out. What a life! Talk about a social security program, here it is. Nothing to do but accept the dole.

But God did not intend it to be forever so. He wanted them to go on to Canaan, the land of corn and wine, the land of victory. But that would mean work for Israel. They would have to toil and work to raise their food, dig wells for their water, and then worse than all, they would have to fight the occupants of Canaan and go to war to subdue and drive them out. We can understand, therefore, that they would rather continue in their life of inactivity and ease than go to work and war. But the path of victory *in* Canaan is not obtained by a life of ease. The path of ease and least resistance was back to the barren desert, ending in their carcasses falling in the wilderness without knowing the sweet rest of Canaan and the flush of victory and a reward for work well done. They had trusted God for their salvation; they could not trust Him for victory.

LACK OF TRUST

The reason is given in Hebrews four:

> For unto us was the gospel preached as well as unto them: but the word preached did not profit them, not being mixed with faith [trust] in them that heard it.
>
> For we which have believed do enter into rest, [but] as he [also] said, As I have sworn in my wrath, if they shall enter into my rest (Heb. 4:2, 3).

The "rest" of salvation is free; the "rest" of victory demands work. The rest of victory cannot be attained till after work has been done. Hence the next verse says concerning the seventh day:

> God did rest the seventh day from all his works (Heb. 4:4b).

God did not rest until He had worked. Rest can only follow toil and labor. There are no people so restless as those who do nothing, and so God says to Israel, Arise, get busy. This same good news which was preached to Israel, "Go up and possess the land," was a shadow and a type of our experience. We have been saved, but God wants us to know the rest and peace of being in His perfect will. And so Israel's entering into Canaan pointed to our spiritual possession of all the blessings of Christ. This is clear from the words:

> For if Jesus [Joshua] had given them rest, then would he not afterward have spoken of another day (Heb. 4:8).

Canaan was not the rest of heaven. That is for a future day. There is a rest which is complete, and another for which we must labor.

> Let us labour therefore to enter into that rest (Heb. 4:11).

The chapter begins with, "Let us therefore fear, lest . . . any of you should seem to come short of it" (Heb. 4:1), but the section ends with the remedy for this fear, "Let us labour therefore" (Heb. 4:11).

Have you had the second blessing? Since you have been saved, have you squarely faced the claims of Christ upon your whole life? Or are you still living a narrow, selfish, carnal and relatively fruitless life, saying some stereotyped prayers, reading a verse or two a day of Scripture as a bit of insurance against some unforeseen incident or accident, and going to church on Sunday? Is that all you have for Jesus, who gave His all for you? God will never use you in any great degree until you bestir yourself and become willing to lay your life on the altar for Him.

SAINTS AND DISCIPLES

How graphically these two groups of believers are depicted in the gospels. In response to Jesus' preaching great multitudes were saved. They were those who came to Him and believed, and they will be found in heaven, but what happened to all these converts to Christ while they were on earth? They just dropped from sight. They were never used in any degree. But when Jesus wanted things done He chose a minority of seventy men who were willing to obey Him. These seventy He sent out — only seventy, from among the thousands of others. They had to leave something and pay the price. To these He laid down the conditions of discipleship:

> Behold, I send you forth as sheep in the midst of wolves: be ye therefore wise as serpents, and harmless as doves.
> The disciple is not above his master, nor the servant above his lord.
> And he that taketh not his cross, and followeth after me, is not worthy of me (Matt. 10:16, 24, 38).

This is the price of discipleship. It has nothing to do with salvation. To illustrate this even more pointedly, we turn to just one of the disciples, Peter. Peter heard two separate calls, separated by a period of time. In John one the disciples of John heard him say, "Behold the Lamb of God," and they had come to Jesus and found Him to be the Messiah. One of them was Andrew, and he first thought of his brother, Simon, "And he brought him to Jesus" (John 1:42). This was Simon Peter's first meeting with Jesus. He came *to* Him, and for all practical purposes it was the day of salvation for Simon. He found the "rest" of Matthew 11:28, "Come unto me." He found the peace of Romans 5:1, "Therefore being justified by faith, we have peace with God." But that seems to have been all, for there is no mention of any outward change in the life, occupation, friends or habits of Simon. He had come to Jesus for salvation, but knew nothing of coming *after* Jesus in surrender.

Peter, therefore, received a second call, not to be confused with this first one. When Simon came *to* Jesus, it was at Jordan. John the Baptist was still out of prison and preaching. When the second call came, it was some time later. Notice the time:

> Now after that John was put in prison, Jesus came into Galilee (Mark 1:14).

The time was later; the place was different. Simon Peter was busy with his old job of fishing, and Jesus came and said:

> Come ye after me, I will make you to become fishers of men. And straightway they forsook their nets, and followed him (Mark 1:17, 18).

Peter was a *saint*, but now he became a *disciple*. The word, "disciple," comes from the same root as the word, "discipline." He now accepted the discipline of his Lord, took the yoke and became a follower of Jesus. It cost him something to follow Jesus. Peter forsook his nets. He left the old life behind and followed Jesus.

This is the "rest of Canaan." This is the life of victory and service. Are you a disciple of Christ, or just a saint bound for heaven, enjoying God's social security and unemployment benefits, but unwilling to fight His battles or go to work? God has something better than just enduring your salvation. He wants you to know the joy of service and sacrifice. And it does cost something to be a disciple. Notice Jesus' reply to the man who said, "Master, I will follow thee whithersoever thou goest" (Matt. 8:19):

> The foxes have holes, and the birds of the air have nests; but the Son of man hath not where to lay his head (Matt. 8:20).

He seems to say, Can you pay the price? Do you still want to follow Me? Again He said:

> If any man come to me, and hate not his father, and mother, and wife, and children and brethren, and sisters, yea his own life also, he cannot be my disciple (Luke 14:26).

This has nothing to do with salvation. It is the price of discipleship. And then Jesus continues:

> And whosoever doth not bear his cross, and come after me, cannot be my disciple (Luke 14:27).

Let us not confuse salvation with discipleship, for they are distinctly different. Salvation is a free gift when we come *to* Jesus, but discipleship comes only by sacrifice in following *after* Jesus. Simon Peter was faced with this call to discipleship and left his nets to follow Jesus. Because there is a price attached to following Jesus, there are but a few people who will follow, but these are the ones He used when He was here, and He is the same today. Before you lightly respond to the invitation of the Son, and glibly say, "Where He leads me I will follow," you had better count the cost, for no man who puts his hand to the plow and looks back is fit to reign. If the price were made more plain by zealous evangelists and preachers when urging young folk to dedicate their lives to the service of the Lord, there would be fewer tragedies on the mission field and in Christian service. Under the spell of some dedication service, they come forward singing:

> I surrender all, I surrender all;
> All to Jesus I surrender, I surrender all.

Many do not know in the least what full surrender involves. Before going any farther they should be told what this surrender means, lest under the temporary enthusiasm and elation of the moment they go out with great zeal, only to come back in a few months or years disappointed, disillusioned, disarmed, discouraged and often disqualified for further service. If we would have them count the cost first, the alarming percentage of missionaries and workers who don't hold out would be greatly reduced. Discipleship is not for the weaklings and babes in Christ. It calls for strong, mature men and women, red-blooded and brave, completely dedicated to be faithful unto death, which indeed it may mean.

Now I shall be accused of discouraging Christians from dedicating their lives for service. I am not discouraging anyone, except those who should be discouraged. Discipleship is not a bed of roses. To dedicate one's life to full time Christian service anywhere the Lord may lead is not a Sunday school picnic or a trip abroad or a place for young couples to spend a protracted honeymoon. But to those who mean business and are willing to "labour to enter into that rest," we have the most encouraging news. This we shall see in our next chapter, but just a hint about it here. We have the wonderful, all-powerful promises of God; we have a great, sympathizing High Priest in heaven; we have an infallible Holy Spirit within us; and at the end of the way a special reward, "for if we suffer with him we shall also reign with him." In Matthew 19:27 we read:

> Then answered Peter and said unto him, Behold, we have forsaken all, and followed thee; what shall we have therefore?

Peter was counting the cost. They had forsaken all to follow Jesus, and now the path turned to the Cross (not to the Kingdom as Peter had imagined). As he wondered if it was worthwhile, Jesus gave the assuring answer which should cheer every disciple:

> Verily I say unto you, That ye which have followed me, in the regeneration [at Jesus' coming] when the Son of man shall sit in the throne of his glory, ye also shall sit upon the twelve thrones, judging the twelve tribes of Israel.
>
> And every one that hath forsaken houses, or brethren, or sisters, or father, or mother, or wife, or children, or lands, for my name's sake, shall receive an hundredfold, and shall inherit everlasting life (Matt. 19:28, 29).

Yes, indeed, it is worthwhile to follow Jesus if we keep our eyes on the glory. Then and then only can we say:

> Jesus, I my cross have taken,
> All to leave and follow thee;
> Destitute, despised, forsaken,
> Thou, from hence, my all shall be:
> Perish every fond ambition,
> All I've sought, and hoped, and known;
> Yet how rich is my condition,
> God and Heav'n are still my own!
>
> Let the world despise and leave me,
> They have left my Saviour, too;
> Human hearts and looks deceive me;
> Thou art not, like man, untrue;
> And, while Thou shalt smile upon me,
> God of wisdom, love, and might,
> Foes may hate and friends may shun me;
> Show Thy face, and all is bright.

Wouldst thou also be his disciple?

CHAPTER NINE

Gaining the Crown

> For the word of God is quick, and powerful, and sharper than any twoedged sword, piercing even to the dividing asunder of soul and spirit, and of the joints and marrow, and is a discerner of the thoughts and intents of the heart.
>
> Neither is there any creature that is not manifest in his sight; but all things are naked and opened unto the eyes of him with whom we have to do (Heb. 4:12, 13).

WHAT a strange place for this passage to occur in Hebrews concerning the power of the Word of God. The preceding verse urges us "to labour to enter into the rest" of a dedicated, separated, yielded life. In this entire chapter the born-again believer is reminded not to be satisfied with mere salvation, but to consider the claims of Christ to follow Him in the path of discipleship and service. This means a clean break with the world, a definite yielding to the call, "Follow me, and I will make you to become fishers of men." It, however, can be had only at a cost *to* self and *of* self. It may mean the severing of tenderest ties, the renouncing of precious associations. And so to encourage His followers, He tells them of the power of the Word of God. It is quick (alive) and powerful and contains every provision for ultimate victory. Add to this the presence of the High Priest in heaven, and we can confidently follow Him. The great crying need of today with its shallow, frothy proclamation of a diluted gospel is for servants of Jesus who will not follow the crowd or be swayed by what others think. There is more for the believer than the blessing of mere salvation; there is also the blessing of discipleship. This blessing comes to those who, having been saved, also make a definite commitment of their lives to Him. It is a prerequisite for victorious service.

Simon Peter experienced it when, subsequent to coming to Christ, he took the step to follow Christ. There is probably not a single God-called preacher reading this who will not be able to testify, "I had first of all an experience of salvation, and then there came a time when I was faced with the challenge of full time service, and when I yielded to this call, it opened up the way God had for my life." It was so in my life. It was over a half year after I came to Christ as my Saviour that I heard His call as Lord of my life, for a surrender of my whole being for the ministry of the Gospel. As long as I refused and gave excuses, I was miserable, but when finally I yielded I found a peace I had never known before, a rest quite over and above the "rest" of being saved. I care not how it happens, or how long afterward it happens, or where it happens, I know that it is the crying need of the day in this age of smug and easy preaching and superficiality and shallowness, as though just believing on Jesus settles everything, and there is no more to be gained. If any would offer the excuse that following Jesus is too costly and dear, then remember that *not* following Him is even more costly, for it is impossible to estimate the loss to those who miss out in the reward at the end of the way. The unfounded notion that because we are saved by grace we are released from all responsibility, and it makes no difference how we live, what we do with our talents, or the testimony we bear, is wholly foreign to the Scriptures. *We must all* appear before the Judgment Seat of Christ.

PAUL'S GREAT FEAR

The secret of Paul's great ministry lay in this very fact, that he had his eye on the future gain, and not on the present loss and sacrifice. It was the proper perspective which made him press onward and forward. He looked through the eyes of the future upon the things of the present. Listen to his testimony:

> We are troubled on every side, yet not distressed; we are perplexed, but not in despair;
>
> Persecuted, but not forsaken; cast down, but not destroyed;
>
> Always bearing about in the body the dying of the Lord Jesus, that the life also of Jesus might be made manifest in our body.
>
> For we which live are alway delivered unto death for Jesus' sake that the life also of Jesus might be made manifest in our mortal flesh (II Cor. 4:8-11).

What was the secret of Paul's victory in the midst of all these trials and tribulations? He tells us:

> Knowing that he which raised up the Lord Jesus shall raise up us also by Jesus and shall present us with you (II Cor. 4:14).

He looked beyond the present distress to the resurrection and the time of reward. And in the light of the reward for faithfulness at Jesus' coming, he could cry out:

> For our light affliction, which is but for a moment, worketh for us a far more exceeding and eternal weight of glory;
>
> While we look not at the things which are seen, but at the things which are not seen: for the things which are seen are temporal; but the things which are not seen are eternal (II Cor. 4:17, 18).

Thirty-five years of persecution, scourging, imprisonment, stonings, revilings, poverty and want, are called by Paul a "light affliction which is but for a moment." What was the secret? It is:

> While we look not at the things which are seen, but at the things which are not seen (II Cor. 4:18a).

MAY BE LOST

But there was still another motive for Paul's unrelenting faithfulness. It was the fear of losing his reward. He had no fear of losing his salvation. He could say:

> I know whom I have believed, and am persuaded that he is able to keep that which I have committed unto him against that day (II Tim. 1:12).

But Paul also recognized the subtlety and weakness of the flesh and knew if he took his eyes off Jesus and the reward, even he would go down. For while salvation cannot be lost because it depends on God's faithfulness, discipleship can be lost because it hinges on our faithfulness. Peter lost his discipleship until he was restored. In II John 8 the apostle warns us:

> Look to yourselves, that we lose not those things which we have wrought [done], but that we receive a full reward.

The things we have done may be lost by disobedience and carelessness. Paul compares the Christian life to a race track with prizes for those who endure and run with patience the race set before them.

> Know ye not that they which run in a race run all, but one receiveth the prize? So run, that ye may obtain.
> I therefore so run, not as uncertainly; so fight I, not as one that beateth the air:
> But I keep under my body [literally buffet my body], and bring it into subjection: lest that by any means, when I have preached to others, I myself should be a castaway (I Cor. 9: 24, 26, 27).

Paul was not running to gain heaven, but running for a reward and a prize at the finish line. Failure to follow the training rules, and press on to the end would disqualify him for the crown. The word, "castaway," in no sense implies loss of salvation, but loss of reward. The word is *adokimos* meaning disapproved or disqualified for the prize.

THE BETTER RESURRECTION

This prize at the end of the race will be given at the resurrection to those who have been faithful, when Jesus comes. It will be at the Judgment Seat of Christ. That prize of approval when we meet Jesus will be worth infinitely more than all the things we may have to sacrifice here. They will fade into "light afflictions which are but for a moment." Paul could say:

> But what things were gain to me, those I counted loss for Christ.
> Yea doubtless, I count all things but loss for the excellency of the knowledge of Christ Jesus my Lord: for whom I have suffered the loss of all things, and do count them but dung, that I may win Christ (Phil. 3:7, 8).

Paul did not renounce all these things and despise the suffering of sacrifice and count all but refuse because he was hoping by doing this to earn salvation or to retain his salvation. He knew that was secure. Lest anyone should imagine that he was teaching salvation by works and self-sacrifice he inserts an explanation:

> . . . not having mine own righteousness, which is of the law, but that which is through the faith of Christ, the righteousness which is of God by faith (Phil. 3:9).

Paul wanted this clear, that salvation was wholly apart from anything he had done or would do, but was all of grace, and then he continues by telling *why* he gladly suffered the loss of all things:

> That I may know him, and the power of his resurrection, and the fellowship of his sufferings, being made conformable unto his death (Phil. 3:10).

He did not mean that he might know Him as Saviour. He already knew Him thus (II Tim. 1:12), but he strove to know Jesus in the "fellowship of his sufferings, and the power of his resurrection." And the reason?

> If by any means I might attain unto the resurrection of the dead (Phil. 3:11).

Here Paul gives his reason for relentlessly pressing the battle lest, having almost gained the victory, he should fall by the way. But what does he mean, "if by any means I might attain unto the resurrection"? Is the resurrection from the dead attained by striving, working and enduring unto the end? Certainly not, for all the saints will be raised at Jesus' coming. That is included in our salvation by grace. We can neither gain our resurrection nor forfeit it. What then does Paul mean? He was striving not to be in the first resurrection, for that was settled, but he strove for a special reward at the resurrection of all saints.

The difficulty arises from an inadequate translation of the original. The phrase, the resurrection of the dead, in the Greek is *ek anastasis ek ton nekron. Ek* means out; *anastasis* means resurrection; and *nekron* means dead ones. Freely translated it should be, The "out resurrection" from those who are raised from among the dead. All the saints will be raised at Jesus' coming, but there will be those who shall receive a reward, and others who will be ashamed, disapproved, castaways, and fail of their full reward. Paul's ambition was to belong to that special group in the first resurrection who would be crowned, and not see all his works burned, and he be saved yet so as by fire.

This awful prospect of failing his Lord made him willing to suffer the loss of all things, to know the power of His resurrection, to enter into the sufferings of Christ, yea being made conformable to His death. With his purpose in mind, to be approved of God as a good workman, he says:

> Brethren, I count not myself to have apprehended: but this one thing I do, forgetting those things which are behind [the sufferings and sacrifices for Christ], and reaching forth unto those things which are before [the rewards],
> I press toward the mark [the goal line] for the prize [crown] of God in Christ Jesus (Phil. 3:13, 14).

It is a serious thing to be a victorious Christian. What a solemnizing thought, that after a life of service, a child of God can play the fool and miss the crown. No wonder Paul says, "I put under my body," "I press toward the mark," "I count all things but loss." How sad to see men of God, after a life of fruitful service, yield to the flesh in an unguarded moment, fall into sin, and be put on the shelf and spend their last years in unfruitfulness. It is a thing to be greatly dreaded. Rather than spoil a life of service by carelessness, it were better the Lord should take them home to glory.

WHAT IS OUR DEFENSE?

But it need not be thus, for God has made adequate provision for victory. The incentives which kept Paul faithful to the end are made perfectly clear in the Word. We mention four of them:

1. The approval of his Lord. In the race we are to keep our eyes on Jesus. His commendation, "Well done, thou good and faithful servant," will compensate for every sacrifice made for Him.

2. The example of Jesus. In laying aside every weight and the sin which does so easily beset us, the secret is:

> Looking unto Jesus, the author and finisher of our faith; who for the joy that was set before him endured the cross, despising the shame, and is set down at the right hand of the throne of God (Heb. 12:2).

3. The Word of Jesus. After the admonition, "Let us labour therefore to enter into that rest [the rest of victory]" (Heb. 4:11), the next verse gives the secret of overcoming. The sword of the Spirit is the overcomer's defense. There can be no victory without the Word of God.

4. The all-sufficient assistance of Jesus. We have in Him a High Priest who understands our struggles and lives to intercede, to help, to support by His Word and Spirit. And so Hebrews four closes with:

> Seeing then that we have a great high priest, that is passed into the heavens, Jesus the Son of God, let us hold fast our profession [not possession — He holds that for us].
> For we have not an high priest which cannot be touched with the feeling of our infirmities; but was in all points tempted like as we are, yet without sin (Heb. 4:14, 15).

Are you troubled by these solemn warnings? Does it make you tremble to recall how you have failed? Does your heart cry out for victory and assurance? Then take heart, for here is the answer in the closing verse:

> Let us therefore come boldly unto the throne of grace, that we may obtain mercy [forgiveness for past failures], and find grace to help in time of need [provision for future victory] (Heb. 4:16).

Why not go to Him now, and begin with a clean sheet, and trust Him for the victory?

CHAPTER TEN

Babes in Christ

> And being made perfect, he became the author of eternal salvation unto all them that obey him;
> Called of God an high priest after the order of Melchisedec (Heb. 5:9, 10).

GOD wants His people perfect, holy and clean. This is the goal of our redemption, viz., to be made as perfect as Christ Himself. He has predestinated us to be ultimately "conformed to the image of his son" (Rom. 8:29). This will not be fully realized until Jesus comes, but the process must begin here and continue progressively. And this can only be attained as we utilize the all-sufficient and adequate provision God has made for our sanctification. He has therefore provided a Mediator, a High Priest who ever liveth to make intercession for us. Jesus is not only the Saviour of sinners, but the interceding High Priest for the keeping of the saints. The very fact that we need someone to intercede for us continually at the right hand of God is irrefutable proof that we are not yet perfect and sinless. Our high Priest has one duty, to make intercession for the sins of the people, to apply the cleansing blood. If believers were able to live absolutely perfect lives in sinless perfection, there would be no need for Christ to continually intercede in our behalf.

In our past studies we have seen that salvation is complete and finished for the believer. Heaven is assured and hell is closed to all who have received Christ. But conversion is only the first step, not only toward heaven, but toward the reward. Nothing done or left undone can keep the believer out of heaven or send him to hell. But what he does with this great salvation will determine his victory here and his crown of reward at the Judgment Seat of Christ. Let no one be deceived into believing that just because one is saved by grace, and his home in heaven is assured, that it makes no difference how he lives or what he does with his life. We *must all* appear before the Judgment Seat of Christ to give an account of what we have done with our talents, our time, our money, and all our opportunities for service. If we neglect so great salvation, we shall suffer loss, but the faithful will be crowned. In the light of this we may well cry out, "And who is sufficient for these things?" (II Cor. 2:16). In ourselves we are totally helpless but we can conquer through Christ.

Quite logically, therefore, Hebrews five (which should begin at Hebrews 4:14) introduces us to the High Priest whose function it is to help all those, who in spite of repeated failures, are seeking the goal of spiritual victory for Chrst. In this section we have two men who were high priests of God. They are Aaron, the human high priest, and Melchisedec, the divine high priest. In these two men we find God's perfect provision for stumbling, falling saints who can say with Paul:

> Not as though I had already attained, either were already perfect: but I follow after, if that I may apprehend [lay hold of] that for which also I am apprehended of Christ Jesus (Phil. 3:12).

Paul was "laid hold of" by Christ with perfection as the goal, and Paul bent every effort toward the practical attainment of that which he already positionally possessed in Christ. To attain this we are to "come boldly unto the throne of grace, that we may obtain mercy, and find grace to help in time of need." This work of the High Priest is now elaborated upon in Hebrews five.

> For every high priest taken from among men is ordained for men in things pertaining to God, that he may offer both gifts and sacrifices for sins:
> Who can have compassion on the ignorant, and on them that are out of the way; for that he himself also is compassed with infirmity (Heb. 5:1, 2).

Aaron was a high priest taken from among men. As such he was a type of Jesus, our High Priest in His humanity. But our Saviour was also a High Priest after the *order* of Melchisedec, as well as after the *type* of Aaron. Both were necessary, for Jesus must be both divine and human. He must be God, to have access for us to God. He must be a man to be man's representative. By His eternal Deity He was a Priest after the order of Melchisedec; by His Incarnation He became a Priest after the type of the Aaronic priesthood. This priestly work of Christ is for believers only. It is not for sinners, for a sinner cannot claim Him as Priest until he has received Him as Saviour. The sinner must come first to the Cross. He must stop at the altar first, before he can enter into the holiest, by the new and living way. The priest was ordained to offer gifts and sacrifices for sins. It was in behalf of those who were ignorant. When the Israelite had sinned through ignorance of God's will (Lev. 4) he could come to the priest and claim forgiveness on the basis of the blood of a sacrifice. Further, the intercession was for those that are "out of the way," for those who have fallen into sin and lost their fellowship with God. For such the priest was ordained to provide cleansing and forgiveness. But Aaron the priest could not intercede for others, until he first offered the blood for himself, for he too was imperfect in his humanity. He is "compassed with infirmity" himself (Heb. 5:2).

> And by reason hereof he ought, as for the people, so also for himself, to offer for sins.
> And no man taketh this honour unto himself, but he that is called of God, as was Aaron (Heb. 5:3, 4).

Aaron being a mere man could not be a perfect priest. Hence his services could not actually take away sins, but all of it was only a type of the One who was to come. The Aaronic sacrifices could only "cover" sin for the time being, but they could not be "put away" until the greater Priest, the Lord Jesus, should offer His blood for an everlasting atonement for sin. Jesus must be human to substitute for humans, and this was after the type of Aaron. But He must be more than a man, for man cannot make full provision for forgiveness and so a second priest is introduced — Melchisedec.

> So also Christ glorified not himself to be made an high priest; but he that said unto him, Thou art my Son, to day have I begotten thee.
>
> As he saith also in another place, Thou art a priest for ever after the order of Melchisedec.
>
> Who in the days of his flesh, when he had offered up prayers and supplications with strong crying and tears unto him that was able to save him from death, and was heard in that he feared;
>
> Though he were a Son, yet learned he obedience by the things which he suffered;
>
> And being made perfect, he became the author of eternal salvation unto all them that obey him;
>
> Called of God an high priest after the order of Melchisedec (Heb. 5:5-10).

Jesus Christ as the Son of God was always a Priest from eternity, after the order of Melchisedec, having neither beginning of days nor end of life. But He must be more than the Son of God to redeem sinners. An atonement for sin must be made, and since only man can atone for man's sin, He came to this earth and became a human Priest to sacrifice Himself upon the altar of the Cross. This was after the type and figure of Aaron. First we are pointed to His eternal priesthood and then we are directed to the "days of his flesh." Here He gave Himself as a human sacrifice for humanity. When Aaron brought sacrifice for Israel he must first bring a sacrifice for himself. He must take his place on a level with those for whom he ministered. In all the offerings he must first bring his own sacrifice. So, too, Jesus, before He could atone for our sins, must stoop to the plane of fallen humanity. The Incarnation was as indispensable in the plan of redemption as His eternal Deity. While He had no sin of His own, yet He must stoop to our human level to assume our guilt, and to sacrifice Himself in our behalf. All this was in fulfillment of the Aaronic priesthood. He was tempted (tested) in all points like as we are — yet without sin.

This entailed the penalty of eternal death. We read that He, the sinless One, offered up prayers and supplications with strong crying and tears. Truly this is holy ground: The Son of God crying out in agony with tears and bloody sweat unto the Father,

> Save me from this hour: but for this cause came I unto this hour (John 12:27).

Our Scripture says He prayed "unto him that was able to save him from death, and was heard." This does not mean that Jesus asked to be spared from dying, but he prayed to be saved *out of death*. Not *from*, but *out of*. He was not seeking to avoid the death, but looked forward and beyond to His resurrection, His triumph over death, and out of death. And He was heard, for after three days He arose because He was obedient in His sufferings.

"And being made perfect," the Scripture says. It does not mean that He was imperfect in any point of His character, but He could not be a perfect Redeemer and High Priest without His death and resurrection. So He arose,

> And being made perfect, he became the author of eternal salvation unto all that obey him;
> Called of God an high priest after the order of Melchisedec (Heb. 5:9, 10).

When He had fulfilled the type of Aaron's priestly office on the Cross He was revealed as our eternal interceding Mediator after the order of Melchisedec at His resurrection. Aaron died, his work uncompleted, to be taken up by others who also could not make it perfect until Jesus came and finished it all.

Its Lesson for Us

I trust that in this discussion you have not forgotten the theme of the whole Book of Hebrews, namely the admonition to ourselves to "go on to perfection." God does not want us to be defeated and powerless. He is appealing to believers who had failed to make proper progress, and urges them not to neglect their great salvation, and although saved, come short of the "rest" of service and the victory of faith. These Hebrews had been saved for some time, but were still babes in Christ. The Holy Spirit's complaint against them is:

> When for the time [after all this time] ye ought to be teachers, ye have need that one teach you again which be the first princi- ples of the oracles of God (Heb. 5:12).

In other words, they hadn't even learned their ABC's.

But there is no excuse for such neglect, and it will be judged of the Lord. With all this light and instruction, with the power of the Word to help us, with such an High Priest to forgive and strengthen, with the Holy Spirit to guide, there is absolutely no excuse for remaining in a state of perpetual spiritual in- fancy. No wonder chapter six opens with:

> Therefore leaving the principles [the A B C's] of the doctrine of Christ, let us go on unto perfection [maturity] (Heb. 6:1).

It is time to be promoted from the kindergarten and go on to maturity. But if we fail to heed the warning, and neglect His admonition after so much pleading, and continue in disobedi- ence, God may finally cease dealing with us here, and permit us to harden our hearts as in the provocation to die in the wilder- ness, without ever knowing victory in this life. How tragic the case of those who must thus come under the judgment of God, where having been enlightened and having tasted the heavenly gift, and having been made partakers of the Holy Ghost, they fall away and it becomes impossible to renew them again unto repentance. They would not repent and be cleansed here, so they will have to be cleansed at the Judgment Seat of Christ, with all their works of hay, wood and stubble going up in smoke, and they themselves saved by the skin of their teeth, so as by fire.

It makes me shudder at the very possibility. It makes me cry out to God to keep me from the fate of becoming a castaway. How can we know we have not reached that point where it is impossible to be renewed to repentance? There need be no doubt about it. If the Word of God has cut you deeply and you realize how you have failed, then you are not one of those who have been hardened. If you receive the Word, and earnestly confess your failure and claim His grace, then you are growing in grace and you need have no fear, for His promise is sure:

> If we confess our sins, he is faithful and just to forgive us our sins, and to cleanse us from all unrighteousness (I John 1:9).

But if you brush off these solemn warnings, and imagine this has no application to you as a believer, you may be at the very point of hardening your heart. We cannot escape the implication by applying it to others. If you have felt no prodding and urging of the Spirit after all these warnings, or if you have resented its solemn implications, then I plead with you:

> Take heed, brethren, lest there be in any of you an evil heart of unbelief, in departing from the living God.
>
> But exhort one another daily, while it is called To day; lest any of you be hardened through the deceitfulness of sin (Heb. 3:12, 13).

CHAPTER ELEVEN

The Sin unto Death

> For it is impossible for those who were once enlightened, and have tasted of the heavenly gift, and were made partakers of the Holy Ghost,
>
> And have tasted the good word of God, and the powers of the world to come,
>
> If they shall fall away, to renew them again unto repentance; seeing they crucify to themselves the Son of God afresh, and put him to an open shame (Heb. 6:4-6).

THIS is admittedly one of the most difficult and controversial passages in the entire Bible, and has been the battleground of many a fierce conflict among theologians and Bible students. The sad part of this controversy and difference of opinion is that it has too often been carried on in a spirit of bitterness and condemnation. Instead of "differing in love," with respect for one another's honest opinion, it has been too often characterized by condemnation, name calling, and a breach of fellowship. Beloved, these things ought not to be. We should discuss our differences with the aim of getting light on the Word, but the arguments of theologians too often "generate more heat than light."

A WORD OF WARNING

We make these introductory remarks as a warning to be Christlike in our differences, realizing that none of us have a corner or monopoly on the truth. We, therefore, invite you to follow our exposition of this passage with an open Bible and an open mind. Then, if after having weighed all the Scriptures, you differ with us, let us do so in love. I emphasize this warning, because I am keenly conscious that some things I shall say concerning Hebrews chapters six and ten run counter and contrary to the generally accepted and traditional interpretation. The fear of contradicting traditional dogmas and sectarian views can be a serious hindrance to progressive light and illumination. No human expositor is infallible, and it is a sad and dangerous obstruction to spiritual progress when we are deterred from differing with the age-old errors of tradition because of fear of being called heretics. Jesus was a heretic in the eyes of the official ecclesiastical system of His day. Paul was a heretic in the eyes of the Sanhedrin of which he had been a member.

Two Views

Now I trust we are prepared to re-examine this passage in Hebrews six, free from prejudice and preconceived notions and ideas. In general, there are two sharply conflicting interpretations of this passage. Let us state the passage once more:

> For it is impossible for those who were once enlightened, and have tasted of the heavenly gift, and were made partakers of the Holy Ghost,
> If they shall fall away, to renew them again unto repentance (Heb. 6:4, 6).

Now the first question which arises is this: Were these people about whom the apostle is writing saved or unsaved? They were either one or the other, and on the correct answer depends the correct interpretation. There are first of all those who assert that these people had been saved, but then had "fallen away" or backslidden, and consequently had lost their salvation, and were again unregenerates and unsaved. We call this "falling from grace." It is the teaching that one can be born again and on the way to heaven, and then through some sin or sins, or losing faith, be ultimately lost and go to hell in the end. We shall come back to this later.

But first we must state the opposite view. It is the view that these folks who "were once enlightened" and were "partakers of the Holy Ghost" were not saved at all, and never had been saved. They are said to be Hebrew professors who had made an outward confession of faith, but had never been born again. This is the view of those who teach the eternal security of believers. We can understand why they should, therefore, insist that these folks were never saved, for if they were and then "fell from grace," it would upset their entire doctrine of "once in grace, always in grace."

THE TWO VIEWS

These are the two views commonly held by Bible students. We want to examine both of them, and see if they are in accord with the rest of Scripture. First, will you notice that if this passage teaches that a man can be saved today, and then backslide and lose his salvation, *he never can be saved. He is forever lost.* Notice carefully what it says. "It is *impossible* to renew them again unto repentance." It is *impossible.* Then a person can only be saved *once,* and if he loses that, there is no more hope, and there is no use to invite him to come and confess and be saved again, for it is *impossible.* Now the very people who insist that the persons in Hebrews 6:4-6 were once saved and then lost their salvation, are the very ones who are incessantly inviting backsliders to return, and folks who have lost their salvation to come and be saved again. What a contradiction! Instead, if a person comes to us and says, "I was saved once, but fell away, and I want to be saved again," we should tell him, "Go away, there is no hope for you; it is impossible to renew you again to repentance." This interpretation breaks down completely, and we must look elsewhere for the true meaning.

Examine with me, therefore, the opposite view of the "security" people who believe in the doctrine of "Once in grace, always in grace." (Now remember, we are merely trying to show the true interpretation of the passage, and not condemning either the Arminian or the Calvinist. We respect the sincere convictions of both, and love them as brethren, even though we may differ on many things.) The view of this school of interpretation is concisely stated in the notes on this passage in the Scofield Bible:

> Hebrews 6:4-8 presents the case of Jewish professed believers who halt short of faith in Christ after advancing to the very threshold of salvation, even "going along with" the Holy Spirit in His work of enlightenment and conviction (John 16:8-10). It is not said that they had faith (Page 1295, Footnotes).

This interpretation is followed by almost all fundamental and Calvinistic students.

It is argued that professors may pose as believers and yet not be possessors; for if Hebrews 6:4-8 teaches that a man can be once saved and then lost, he can never repent and be saved again. So there is no use inviting such an one to come back to Christ, since it is impossible for him to repent. As someone has said, You have a through pass to perdition.

For this reason our good friends reject this interpretation and insist that these folks never were saved at all. They were mere professors and not possessors. But that presents the same difficulty. Remember, it says of these that it is *impossible* to renew them to repentance. Do we believe that if a man has been a false professor, a mere church member, a religious hypocrite, there is no chance for him to be saved? Is it true that if a person has once made a profession of Christ, but later it proves to be not genuine, there is no hope for such an one to ever be saved? It would be difficult to reconcile this with the invitation of the Gospel, and the message of "whosoever will may come." We have all seen hundreds, yea, thousands, who formerly had been religious professors, but had gone into sin, then have come to Christ and found Him as willing to forgive as He is to any other.

What Is the Answer?

Who then is right? There is an element of truth in both views, but both miss the point entirely. The writer of Hebrews six is not talking about losing salvation. He is talking about repentance. It does not say, "It is impossible to renew them unto

salvation." What a gloomy Gospel it would be — telling people
in this day of grace that it is impossible for them to be saved.
I trust you have followed us thus far. As we study the context
of the entire epistle we must conclude that the author is writing
to believers who have been born again. This is evident from the
many fruits of the Spirit which had been present in their lives.
Moreover, these believers had been saved a long time, and had
progressed far on the way of Christian growth. And then they
had lost their first love and instead of going forward, they began
to fall behind. We repeat, without apology the "heart" of Hebrews in chapter five:

> For when for the time ye ought to be teachers, ye have need
> that one teach you again which be the first principles of the ora-
> cles of God; and [ye] are become such as have need of milk, and
> not of strong meat (Heb. 5:12).

These folks should have been mature, but instead they had
lapsed into spiritual infancy, and so the apostle opens the sixth
chapter of Hebrews with this plea:

> Therefore leaving the principles [the A B C's, the baby food]
> of the doctrine of Christ, let us go on unto perfection (Heb. 6:1).

The word "perfection" means maturity. It is so used also in
Luke 8:14, where the seed among thorns is said to "bring no
fruit to perfection [maturity]."

And then follows the dire warning of our Scripture. It is
possible for a believer who has gone a long way on the path of
service, to fall by the wayside, and as a result the Lord in
chastening sets his ministry aside and he becomes one of God's
"castaways." He is not lost, but his usefulness is ended, and
he will have to bear his judgment at the Judgment Seat of
Christ, when all the believer's works shall be tried with fire.
This is the meaning of Paul's words in I Corinthians three:

> If any man's work shall be burned, he shall suffer loss: for he
> himself shall be saved; yet so as by fire (I Cor. 3:15).

This was the thing Paul feared above all things. Paul did
not fear losing his salvation. He was sure of that, but he feared

losing out on the reward and the crown. He feared that after a lifetime of preaching he might in a careless moment succumb to the flesh and be set aside. That he did not fear losing his salvation is clear. He says:

> . . . I know whom I have believed, and am persuaded that he is able to keep that which I have committed unto him against that day (II Tim. 1:12).

But there was something Paul did fear. He says in I Corinthians nine:

> Know ye not that they which run in a race run all, but one receiveth the prize? So run, that ye may obtain.
>
> I therefore so run, not as uncertainly; so fight I, not as one that beateth the air:
>
> But I keep under my body, and bring it into subjection: lest that by any means, when I have preached to others, I myself should be a castaway (I Cor. 9:24, 26, 27).

How this passage has confused people! But notice carefully, Paul is *not* talking about salvation, but about rewards and a crown for faithfulness. He is talking about "running a race." Surely the sinner must not run to get into heaven or to obtain salvation. That is a free gift. A dead sinner cannot run.

Paul knew better. He knew salvation did not depend on our running, but upon the grace of God. What Paul feared was that after a life of service, he might play the fool, lose out on the reward and make it necessary for God to put him on the shelf. It is possible for a Christian to fall away until God "retires" him from service, waiting to deal with him at the Judgment Seat of Christ, to see all the wood, hay and stubble go up in smoke, and he be saved "so as by fire."

The word "castaway" is translated in the Revised Version as "rejected." It means "disqualified to receive a reward." Again let me remind you, Paul is *not* thinking of salvation, but of earning a crown. Sinners are not in a race; only Christians run for the prize. He expresses the same ambition in Philippians three:

> Brethren, I count not myself to have apprehended: but this
> one thing I do, forgetting those things which are behind, and
> reaching forth unto those things which are before,
> I press toward the mark [finish line, the goal] for the prize
> [crown] of the high calling of God in Christ Jesus (Phil. 3:13, 14).

This, we believe, will explain the passage in Hebrews six. He is speaking of Christians who began the race, but fell by the wayside. There comes a time when after repeated warnings and admonitions the Christian continues in disobedience and "willful" sin, until God shelves him, to deal with him at the Judgment Seat of Christ. The passage refers to the sin unto death, the result of presumptuous, willful, continued disobedience against better light. Such may never repent here below, but be among those who shall be "ashamed at His appearing."

It is a serious thing to be a child of God. It carries grave responsibilities; and willful continuance in known sin against clear and better light must call for the chastening of the Lord. The Bible admonishes us:

> Let a man examine himself . . .
> For if we would judge ourselves, we should not be judged.
> But when we are judged, we are chastened of the Lord, that
> we should not be condemned with the world (I Cor. 11:28,
> 31, 32).

CHAPTER TWELVE

God's Castaways

IS it true that the Bible teaching of grace and security leads to carelessness and license? What about Christians who have been truly born again and then fall into sin? What about some who apparently were saved, but fall away and die without giving evidence of repentance? Is it true that when we are saved, and all our sins, past, present and future, are put under the blood, it will then make no difference how we live? These are questions of grave import and are constantly asked; therefore we should be able to give an answer. Various groups have sought to answer the question: What is God going to do with believers who fall into sin and die before repenting? The Catholic Church has its answer in "purgatory." The Arminians have their answer in "falling from grace," and they say that such believers are lost again. Certain holiness groups have another answer. They say that only the "sanctified" ones will be raptured when Jesus comes, and the others will have to pass through the Tribulation. Now these are all attempts to answer the question: What happens to believers who die in unconfessed sin? Well, I hear some of you say, "I don't believe any of those explanations are correct." But let me ask you, Do you have a better answer? Or have you an answer at all? Before rejecting any solution, you should have a better one to replace it. We should never reject someone else's interpretation unless we can give a better one.

We certainly cannot accept a doctrine which teaches that God will do nothing about it. Common sense as well as the Bible teaches that we cannot claim to be Christians and continue in sin. We would re-examine this problem in the light of Scripture. Our first definite proposition is that God does hold believers accountable. In I Corinthians eleven Paul teaches that because believers will not judge sin in their own lives, God visits them with chastening, which may take various forms.

> For this cause many are weak and sickly among you, and many sleep (I Cor. 11:30).

Living in known, willful sin and disobedience will bring physical chastening in the form of weakness and sickness. If this chastening fails to correct, God may take that child of His by death, to be straightened out at the Judgment Seat of Christ. In the same vein, the writer of Hebrews says in Hebrews twelve:

> Now no chastening for the present seemeth to be joyous, but grievous: nevertheless, afterward it yieldeth the peaceable fruit of righteousness unto them which are exercised thereby (Heb. 12:11).

Notice the last phrase,

> It yieldeth [worketh] the peaceable fruit of righteousness *to them which are exercised thereby.*

But what about those who are *not* exercised thereby, those who, instead of repenting and returning under the chastening of the Lord, become bitter and rebellious, and continue in their disobedience? With such God deals in a different way. He may either take them by death (I Cor. 11:30) or cease dealing with them here, and take them out of service, putting them on the shelf. These are the folks referred to in that controversial passage in Hebrews six, which because of its importance we quote once again:

> For it is impossible . . .
> If they shall fall away, to renew them again unto repentance (Heb. 6:4, 6).

It is definitely not a matter of salvation, but a matter of chastening; not condemnation but judgment of their sins. It is a solemn warning against the "sin unto death." The epistle has many such warnings. In Hebrews 2:1 the apostle, speaking to believers says:

> Therefore we [the writer includes himself as a believer] ought to give the more earnest heed to the things which we have heard, lest at any time we should let them slip.

Or consider the opening verse in chapter four:

> Let us [again the writer includes himself] therefore fear, lest a promise being left us of entering into his rest, any of you should seem to come short of it (Heb. 4:1).

This warning again is not against losing salvation, but coming short of the "rest" of the believer's victory. There are two kinds of rest, sharply distinguished in the Scriptures. There is a "rest" of salvation, which is God's free gift; and a "rest" of service, for which we must labor. The one is the rest of salvation; the other is the rest of reward.

BELIEVERS CAN FALL SHORT

Now with this twofold possibility of Christian experience in view, turn again to Hebrews six. The whole Book of Hebrews is written to believers, and has to do with their rewards, and not salvation. They are called "holy brethren" in Hebrews 3:1. They have a great High Priest (Heb. 4:15). They are admonished to come "boldly" unto the throne of grace (Heb. 4:16). But the all-conclusive evidence about the people addressed in Hebrews 6:4-12 is found in the description of these believers. Notice carefully of whom it is said to be impossible to renew to repentance, if they fall away. It is said they:

> . . . were once enlightened, and have tasted of the heavenly gift, and were made partakers of the Holy Ghost,
> And have tasted the good word of God, and the powers of the world to come (Heb. 6:4, 5).

If that is not a description of true, born-again believers, then language means nothing, and we cannot understand anything in the Word of God any more. Five marks of the believer are given:

1. They were once enlightened.
2. They had tasted the heavenly gift.
3. They were partakers of the Holy Ghost.
4. They had tasted the good Word of God.
5. They had knowledge of prophecy.

The exponents of the doctrine that these people were not truly saved, but were mere professors, have attempted an answer to this description, but it fails to stand under examination. They tell us that unconverted sinners do see the light of the Gospel, they taste the heavenly gift and the good Word of God, but have never appropriated or "eaten" it. Being "partakers" of the Holy Ghost is made to mean that they did not actually possess the Holy Spirit, but had merely "gone along with" Him in an outward profession.

COMPARE SCRIPTURE WITH SCRIPTURE

Is this argument defensible in the light of other Scripture? What do these words, "enlightened," "tasted," "partakers," mean when used elsewhere in the Bible? If we know this, then we shall be able to know what the Holy Spirit means in this passage.

First then the meaning of the word, "enlightened." It is the translation of the Greek word, *photizo,* and means to "make to see." The word is translated twice as enlightened (Eph. 1:18; Heb. 6:4) and once as illuminated (Heb. 10:32). What is its meaning in Ephesians 1:18?

> The eyes of your understanding being enlightened; that ye may know what is the hope of his calling, and what the riches of the glory of his inheritance in the saints.

In the one other instance where the word is used we read:

> But call to remembrance the former days, in which, after ye were illuminated [the same word], ye endured a great fight of afflictions (Heb. 10:32).

In both references the application is strictly to born-again people. By what rule of interpretation then can we say that in Hebrews 6:4 it does not mean "to see"? Can an unregenerate sinner see the riches of His glory? If he can, then Jesus was wrong when He said, "Except a man be born again, he cannot see . . ." (John 3:3).

TASTE AND SEE

The word, "taste," in our Scripture is *genomai* in the Greek and means to experience and to eat. This is its meaning whereever else it is used. It occurs once earlier in Hebrews 2:9 and says that Jesus

> . . . by the grace of God should taste death for every man.

The same word is used. Does it mean to taste only, and not partake of it? As one Bible teacher says, "It is one thing to taste — another to eat." To what pains men will go to defend their theories. The same word, *genomai*, is used in I Peter:

> As newborn babes, desire the sincere milk of the word, that ye may grow thereby:
> If so be ye have tasted that the Lord is gracious (I Pet. 2:2, 3).

The meaning of the word is clear from these other passages. By no method of reasoning then can we say that in Hebrews six it means to "touch" but not to appropriate.

PARTAKERS OF THE HOLY GHOST

But in addition we are told that these people were "partakers of the Holy Ghost." This is made to mean that they had agreed with and gone along with the Holy Spirit, but had never received Him. As one has put it, "They were neither sealed nor indwelt nor baptized nor filled with the Spirit." Just because it does not go into detail means nothing. These operations simply are not mentioned, because all of them are implied in being partakers. But we submit the following unassailable proof that these people were indwelt by the Holy Spirit as born-again believers:

The word "partakers" is *metochos* in the original. It is translated "partakers" in five passages (Heb. 3:1; 3:14; 6:4; 12:8; and 12:10). It is translated "fellows" once (Heb. 1:9).

We need do little more than quote the passages where it occurs to see the real meaning of the word.

> Wherefore, holy brethren, partakers of the heavenly calling, consider the Apostle and High Priest of our profession, Christ Jesus (Heb. 3:1).

> For we are made partakers of Christ if we hold the beginning of our confidence stedfast unto the end (Heb. 3:14).

> But if ye be without chastisement, whereof all are partakers (Heb. 12:8).

> . . . that we might be partakers of his holiness (Heb. 12:10b).

In addition to these, the word is used in a few other passages, but all with the same meaning — to participate, to be part of. In Hebrews 1:9 Jesus is said to be anointed with the oil of gladness above His fellows. The word "fellows" is a translation of the same word as "partakers."

In I Corinthians 9:10 we are said to be "partaker[s] of his hope." In II Timothy 2:6 a slightly different form is used, but the meaning is the same.

> The husbandman that laboureth must be first partaker of the fruits.

See also I Corinthians 10:17; I Peter 4:13; II Peter 1:4. In every instance it means to share to the fullest extent.

Now we have left our verse in Hebrews 6:4. Here it is stated that partakers of the Holy Spirit can fall away. By what rule of interpretation can this be construed as not being full participants? An illustration follows. The same soil can bring forth fruit or briers. If the soil is cultivated, it will produce fruit; if it is neglected, it will produce briers. The same good seed in Mark five fell on good ground, yet some yielded only thirtyfold, other sixtyfold, and only a small part of it one hundredfold. Every man's work shall be tried with fire, and the "briers" of neglect and disobedience go up in smoke. But the apostle hopes his warning will take effect and trusts that they will bring forth fruits that "accompany salvation." God says He will remember their work and labour of love, which ye have shewed toward his name, in that ye have ministered to the saints, and do minister (Heb. 6:10).

And then he clinches it in verse eleven, and says:

And we desire that every one of you do shew the same diligence to the full assurance of hope unto the end (Heb. 6:11).

Obedience and self-judgment and faithfulness and diligence in our service will result in full assurance. It is not a matter of salvation, but of reward and assurance and fruit, and the final approval of His "Well done, thou good and faithful servant." Christian, walk carefully, with your eye on the goal. How fitting the conclusion of this passage:

That ye be not slothful, but followers of them who through faith and patience inherit the promises (Heb. 6:12).

Examine yourself, judge every known and doubtful sin, confess to Him, and be clean, and you need never fear the judgment, against which we are so earnestly warned.

CHAPTER THIRTEEN

The Heavenly Priesthood

THE Book of Hebrews is a book of solemn warnings. Throughout its thirteen chapters are numerous admonitions and danger signals. These Hebrew Christians were in a difficult situation, having been saved out of Judaism. It meant a tremendous sacrifice, for confessing Christ meant a virtual severing of all ties with their former fellows and associates. They were now identified with a most despised group called Christians, who were considered a sect of fanatics and the offscouring of the earth. To make a clean break with their old religion and its social implications was not easy. As a result they were tempted to compromise their position, and to straddle the fence, with one foot in the law and the other in grace. As a result they made no progress, and were in danger of losing their joy, testimony and reward.

Against this danger the epistle warns them in no uncertain terms. They are warned not to neglect their great salvation, or come short of victory, but to hold fast their confidence and go on to perfection. The incentive is the commendation of the Lord and the promise of future reward. The means for attaining the victory are the example of Jesus, the power of the Word, the availability of the services of the Holy Spirit, and of the High Priest at the right hand of God. But there is also a penalty attached for failure to obey. It invites the chastening of the Lord (fully developed in chapter twelve of this book) and in the event that this chastening is "despised" (Heb. 12:5), the Lord may take a still sterner course, and set them aside as "castaways" to be dealt with at the Judgment Seat of Christ.

109

This we saw was implied in the words that "it is impossible to renew them again unto repentance."

NOT MATTER OF SALVATION

It is not a matter of salvation, but rewards. When the Christian fails, and continues in unrepentance, God does not cast him off, but rather seeks to restore him. This is accomplished by the Word, repeated warnings, and if these are ignored, by chastening which may take the form of weakness, sickness and even death (I Cor. 11:30). This is a solemn revelation, that if the Christian is not exercised by chastening and brought to repentance, the Lord may then remove such an one by death, to receive his proper cleansing at the Judgment Seat. Does this alarm you? Do you resent it and find it hard to believe that God would deal so severely with His children? Ask yourself, what other course can He take? It is infinitely better that God should chasten us for our mistakes, no matter how severe that chastening, than that He should cast us off and send us back to hell. I am inexpressibly thankful to God that when we fall and fail, He does not disown us as His children and cause us to lose our salvation, but instead will use even the severest means to restore us again that we "should not be condemned with the world" (I Cor. 11:23). Ask yourself which you would prefer, to be judged by God in correcting you by chastening and suffering loss at the Judgment Seat in order that you may be cleansed, or to be abandoned to everlasting punishment in the lake of fire? The answer should be easy; it is infinitely better to suffer any degree of chastening for a little time only, than to spend eternity in hell. I am thankful that He loves me so much that He will not let me go, but will go to the extremest measures in correcting me.

EXAMPLE OF ABRAHAM

This glorious truth is next set forth in Hebrews 6:13-19. After warning the believer against falling away to the point where it is impossible to be renewed to repentance, he hastens to add that this does not mean loss of salvation, but deals with God's method of finally cleansing the believer. To illustrate this security in spite of our failures, he introduces God's dealing with father Abraham. He has urged these believers to be diligent to maintain their assurance and hope (not salvation) unto the end (Heb. 6:22), and through faith and patience inherit the rewards (Heb. 6:12). The incentive for this is God's faithfulness in spite of our unfaithfulness, as seen in God's dealings with Abraham.

> For when God made promise to Abraham, because he could swear by no greater, he sware by himself,
> Saying, Surely blessing I will bless thee, and multiplying I will multiply thee (Heb. 6:13, 14).

God promised to do something for Abraham. It did not depend on Abraham's worth, merit, works or conduct, but only on God's promise, and so He covenants with Himself to do it. Nothing could altar this purpose in grace, and so the writer adds:

> And so, after he had patiently endured, he obtained the promise (Heb. 6:15).

The possession of God's promise to Abraham depended on God's faithfulness. The enjoyment and assurance of the promise rested upon Abraham's faithfulness. And God confirmed the promise:

> Wherein God, willing more abundantly to shew unto the heirs of promise the immutability [unchangeableness] of his counsel, confirmed it by an oath:
> That by two immutable things, in which it was impossible for God to lie, we might have a strong consolation, who have fled for refuge to lay hold upon the hope set before us:
> Which hope we have as an anchor of the soul, both sure and stedfast, and which entereth into that within the veil (Heb. 6:17-19).

Blessed assurance! "If we believe not, yet he abideth faithful: he cannot deny himself" (II Tim. 2:13).

God has promised and He cannot fail. When we fail, therefore, this then is the impelling motive for repentance, that God has made provision for our restoration and cleansing. This promise of God's faithfulness is compared to an anchor gripping the rock. We may be buffeted and dashed about by the storms, but our anchor is secure. The reason is given — it is anchored within the veil — in the most Holy Place where the Priest has sprinkled the blood upon the mercy seat. Our salvation is anchored by the Priest with the precious blood within the veil.

> Whither the forerunner is for us entered, even Jesus, made an high priest for ever after the order of Melchisedec (Heb. 6:20).

The next three chapters of Hebrews are a parenthesis between two solemn warnings found in chapters six and ten. The warning in the former is against falling away (Heb. 6:4-12), and the warning in Hebrews 10:26-39 is against willful sinning. Between these two solemn passages the Holy Spirit has inserted three chapters on the perfect, complete, enduring, intercessory work of our High Priest, Jesus, at the right hand of God. The reason for this arrangement is clear. In these parenthetical chapters we have God's own provision against our "falling away" and reaching a place where it is "impossible to be renewed again unto repentance." Jesus is offering forgiveness, and promises to supply grace to keep us, if we will but avail ourselves of His service and "come boldly unto the throne of grace."

The solemn implications of the judgment in chapters six and ten might indeed discourage us and cause us to despair, or even lead us to believe we had again lost our salvation. And so this graphic picture of the merciful High Priest is inserted between these two solemn warnings. He is the One who can help us, forgive and restore us and keep us. If you fear that you have committed the sins mentioned in Hebrews six and ten, and you fear you are a castaway, you can know whether you have, or have not, by going to Him in repentance. If you confess your sin, and seek His mercy, then you have not committed the "sin unto death," since for such it is "impossible to renew them to repentance." Those who are guilty of the great transgression have no more sense of conviction, but have been hardened. Be assured that God's promise is true,

> If we confess our sins, he is faithful and just to forgive us our sins, and to cleanse us from all unrighteousness (I John 1:9).

LOOK TO THE PRIEST

We come now to the three chapters on the High Priest and His work in behalf of His people. First our attention is called to the mysterious king-priest, Melchisedec. We do not know a great deal about him. All that is recorded of him is found in the brief passages in Genesis (14) and Psalms (110) and in Hebrews. Various guesses have been made as to the identity of this mysterious character. Some believe he was a Christophany, a corporeal appearing of Jesus Himself. Others believe he was some supernatural messenger; others that he was Shem, the son of Noah, or some mighty angel, or some other person who was a type of the priesthood of Christ. We need not speculate, for this man was either an appearing of Jesus Himself in human form, or a type of the Lord. The name means king of righteousness, and he was the king of peace (Heb. 7:2). His ancestry is shrouded in mystery, without father or mother, without beginning of days and without end of life. He was made like unto the son of God and represents the eternal priesthood of Christ. He "abideth a priest continually."

WHY IS HE INTRODUCED?

But why is he introduced at all? Here in Hebrews he is mentioned to assure us that we can have victory and avoid failing to achieve God's best for us, because we have a High Priest who lives for the very purpose of giving us the victory. But the record in Genesis fourteen gives an even clearer reason for Melchisedec's appearing on the scene.

While Lot was living in Sodom, the city was attacked and taken by the armies of four powerful kings. They captured the king of Sodom, and also Abraham's nephew Lot and his family. Abraham, hearing about Lot's disaster, magnanimously mustered a little army of 318 trained servants and gained a mighty victory, recovering all the spoils of Sodom, and delivering Lot and his family. According to the rules of war "to the victor belongs the spoils," and so Abraham had a legal right to take the spoils for himself. But it would have ruined his testimony if he had yielded to the temptation of enriching himself through the misfortune of others. This must have been a great temptation for him. He might try to justify his action, but the moral effect of his testimony would be ruined. God knew Abraham's weakness, and the danger of yielding to this opportunity of greatly profiting materially. And so God sends help in the person of Melchisedec, the priest of the Most High.

> And Melchizedek king of Salem brought forth bread and wine . . . .
> And he blessed him, and said, Blessed be Abram of the most high God, possessor of heaven and earth:
> And blessed be the most high God, which hath delivered thine enemies into thy hand. And he [Abraham] gave him tithes of all (Gen. 14:18-20).

As Abraham faces this great temptation to gain material profit at the expense of his testimony, God sends His high priest to remind Abraham that he does not need the patronage of the world, and has no need to depend on questionable deals to enrich himself. You have something far better, Melchisedec seems to say. You have God as your patron and provider. Notice how Abraham is reminded of this. Melchisedec says, "Blessed be Abram of the most high God, possessor of heaven and earth." Are you looking with longing eyes at the perishable spoils of Sodom, the worthless trinkets of the world? You don't need them, Abraham, you have God, the possessor of heaven and earth. He owns the cattle upon a thousand hills.

Then Abraham is reminded that he did not win the battle, but God, for he says:

> Blessed be the most high God, which hath delivered thine enemies into thy hand (Gen. 14:20).

These spoils are not yours; they belong to Me. Only trust Me, refuse the paltry offer of the king of Sodom, and I will reward you far above any seeming sacrifice you may make. The help was accepted and Abraham gave his tithe to God's priest. Then when the king of Sodom came and said, "Give me the persons and take the goods for thyself," Abraham was able to answer:

> . . . I have lift up mine hand unto . . . the possessor of heaven and earth,
> That I will not take from a thread even to a shoelatchet . . . lest thou shouldest say, I have made Abram rich (Gen. 14:22, 23).

VICTORY, VICTORY

Abraham had gained a greater victory than the one over the four mighty kings. He had gained the victory over *Abraham*. He had conquered self and surrendered it to God. And now comes the reward, for:

> After these things the word of the LORD came unto Abram . . . saying, Fear not, Abram: I am thy shield, and thy exceeding great reward (Gen. 15:1).

Our great High Priest in heaven lives to do the same thing for us. When we are tempted to accept the patronage of the world, He reminds us we do not need the friendship of unbelievers, for we have Him. As Melchisedec brought forth bread and wine to strengthen Abraham, so He has given us the Lord's Supper as the memorial of His victorious death and resurrection. To us it often seems that we must cooperate with the world and compromise with unbelievers if we are to succeed. To take a separated stand for Christ may mean loss of popularity, of material things, even poverty or bankruptcy. We are tempted to tolerate the evil practices of the world, to indulge in some borderline, shady practices, to excuse some questionable social or business practices to keep our customers, water down our testimony for fear of offending those whom we feel can be of some help to us. But God says, *no!* Trust Me, be out-and-out for Me, and touch not the unclean thing. It may seem that the cost of a separated walk is too high, but if we dare to trust Him,

He will not fail but will reward us with blessings here and by and by, which will make all our sacrifices here seem like worthless trinkets and toys which break into fragments at our touch. Do you, child of God, dare to trust Him today, refuse to compromise, refuse the patronage of the world, no matter how great the immediate advantage may seem to be? Then you will be able to sing:

> Take the World, but give me Jesus,
>   All its joys are but a name;
> But His love abideth ever,
>   Thro' eternal years the same.

Let your conversation be without covetousness; and be content with such things as ye have: for he hath said, I will never leave thee, nor forsake thee.

So that we may boldly say, The Lord is my helper, and I will not fear what man shall do unto me (Heb. 13:5, 6).

CHAPTER FOURTEEN

The Price of Discipleship

> For the law made nothing perfect, but the bringing in of a better hope did (Heb. 7:19).

THERE is a vast difference between coming *to* Jesus for salvation, and coming *after* Jesus for service. Coming to Christ makes one a believer, while coming after Christ makes one a disciple. All believers are not disciples. To become a believer one accepts the invitation of the Gospel; to be a disciple one obeys the challenge to a life of dedicated service and separation. Salvation comes through the sacrifice of Christ; discipleship comes only by sacrifice of self and surrender to His call for devoted service. Salvation is free, but discipleship involves paying the price of a separated walk. Salvation cannot be lost because it depends upon God's faithfulness, but discipleship can be lost because it depends upon our faithfulness.

The Lord Jesus does not desire that we should merely seek to make believers out of sinners, but wants us to make disciples out of saints. Preaching results in believers, but only by teaching the saints can we make them disciples. We have, therefore, two commissions which our Lord left us before He went away. They are found in Mark sixteen and Matthew twenty-eight. The first is familiar to all:

> Go ye into all the world, and preach the gospel to every creature.
> He that believeth and is baptized shall be saved; but he that believeth not shall be damned (Mark 16:15, 16).

117

This is the commission to evangelize. The other commission is not so well known, and seems to be largely forgotten in these days of popular evangelism. To many, just being saved, escaping hell, and going to heaven, seems to be the sum total of salvation. But God wants us to go on to the full enjoyment and maturity of our Christian experience. We have, therefore, in Matthew a different commission, just as binding upon us as the one already mentioned.

> And Jesus came and spake unto them, saying, All power is given unto me in heaven and in earth.
>
> Go ye therefore, and teach [disciple] all nations, baptizing them in the name of the Father, and of the Son, and of the Holy Ghost:
>
> Teaching them to observe [obey] all things whatsoever I have commanded you: and, lo, I am with you alway, even unto the end of the world. Amen (Matt. 28:18-20).

This order is quite different from the command to preach the message of salvation in Mark sixteen. Notice a number of things about this commission in Matthew twenty-eight.

1. This commission is associated with *power* for service. Jesus says, *"All* power is given unto me, *go ye therefore."* Obedience to this commission results in power. A person may be a "powerless" believer, but for discipleship power is an absolute requisite.

2. The object is not to make believers by preaching, but to make disciples by *teaching.* The word "teach" in verse nineteen means "to make disciples." To make disciples, instruction is indispensable. Disciples are believers who are *taught* in the Word. It is the same truth as taught in Matthew 11:29, "Take my yoke upon you, and learn of me." If you want to be a disciple, you must spend much time with the Teacher and study the lesson of the Word diligently.

3. Discipleship emphasizes implicit *obedience.* In salvation the emphasis is on *faith* as the one prerequisite, but to be a disciple one must observe [obey] all things whatsoever I have commanded you (Matt. 28:20).

THE BURDEN OF HEBREWS

This lesson of obedience is the burden of the Book of Hebrews. The people to whom it was written were still "babes in Christ," undeveloped and immature. They were believers, but knew little about discipleship. Hence the central theme of Hebrews is:

> For when . . . ye ought to be teachers [disciples], ye have need that one teach you again . . . and are become such as have need of milk (Heb. 5:12).

They were merely believers, but should strive to become mature disciples, able to partake of the solid meat of the Word. Hence the advice:

> Therefore leaving the principles of the doctrine of Christ, let us go on unto perfection [maturity] (Heb. 6:1).

SACRIFICE AND SEPARATION

But this discipleship entailed a great sacrifice. For these Hebrews to receive Christ was a tremendous step which we can hardly appreciate today, when to be a Christian is quite the popular thing. But in those days it meant associating one's self with a despised group, leaving behind many precious traditions and associations, and taking a stand for Christ "without the camp." They had been members of a proud and favored nation, with a miraculous history and precious traditions. They were Israelites, members of the chosen nation, with a most impressive religion of rituals, ceremonies and worship. They were familiar with the solemn feast days, the Passover, the Day of Atonement and unleavened bread. They had been zealous in their religion, and were associated with the most cultured and religious people of their day.

But once they received Christ and aligned themselves with the Church, all this must be left behind. No more worship in the temple, no more jubilation with the crowd as the sacrificial lambs were offered, no more feasting with the religious worshipers in the Temple and synagogue. All this was over now, for all had been fulfilled in Christ. He said, "It is finished," and the shadows gave way to the substance. The sacrifice of animals, the pouring out of animal blood, the worship in the Temple and the ministry of the priests was now all an empty mockery, now that Christ had died and arisen. The veil had been rent, the old economy had passed, being fulfilled once for all in Christ.

HARD TO LEAVE

The great mass of Israel, however, did not know this, and continued in their impressive, stately, ritualistic, but empty religious activities. To the Christians this was all an empty show, but was nevertheless difficult to leave behind. Now they had no impressive ritual, no beautiful temple, no beautifully garbed priesthood, and the temptation to go back into the legal formalism of Judaism must have been strong. If they would only compromise a little, it would be much easier. But to do so would mean losing the power of discipleship, losing rewards, inviting the chastening of the Lord. It is to prevent this that the severe warnings in Hebrews six and ten are given. In Hebrews seven to nine we have, therefore, a comparison of the old legal system and their new liberty in grace. By comparing the two, the contrast is made all the more striking. Once we see how much better grace is than law, how much better to follow Christ even to the Cross, than to go back to the easy path of least resistance and popularity, we shall be able to *go on to maturity.*

Time prevents an exhaustive verse-by-verse exposition of Hebrews chapters seven, eight, nine and part of ten. Others have adequately dealt with the subject. The whole section is devoted to showing how far superior grace is to law, how much better Christ is than the shadows of Him in the Old Testament. It sets forth the priesthood of Christ as infinitely superior to the priesthood of Aaron, and the blood of Christ over the blood of animal sacrifices. These chapters (seven, eight and nine) may be divided under the following headings. Christ is superior to and better than:

1. The priesthood of Aaron (ch. 7).
2. The Tabernacle in the wilderness (ch. 8:1-6).
3. The old covenant of the law (ch. 8:7-13).
4. All the sacrifices under the law (ch. 9:1-15).
5. All the blood of all the sacrificial animals (ch. 9:15-28).

All this was designed to encourage the Hebrew Christians to forsake the shadows and follow Christ, the Substance, to the end.

BETTER THAN AARON

First then it is shown that the priesthood of Christ was better than Aaron's. Aaron's priestly ministry was imperfect, because he himself was a sinner and needed to sacrifice for himself. Moreover the priesthood under the law was incomplete, for the priest died before he had finished his work, and it had to be continued by his successors. The priesthood of Aaron was not from the tribe of Judah, but Levi, while God's eternal Priest was to be of the kingly line of Judah. The only acceptable priest must also be a king. In Israel no king was allowed to be a priest, and no priest was allowed to be a king. But in Christ both are combined, and therefore, He was after the order of Melchisedec, who was "King of righteousness," and a "priest of the most high God."

The argument is summed up in these words:

> And they truly were many priests, because they were not suffered to continue by reason of death:
>
> But this man [Jesus], because he continueth ever, hath an unchangeable priesthood.
>
> Wherefore he is able also to save them to the uttermost that come unto God by him, seeing he ever liveth to make intercession for them (Heb. 7:23-25).

O ye Hebrews, the author seems to say, why look back to the old religion of the law when you have something much better in Christ? And we would cry, O you Christians of today, why aren't you satisfied with Christ? Why look back to the old life, and cling to the things of religion and the law? Why, like Israel, will you lust after the flesh pots of Egypt, the onions, leeks and garlic of the world? Grow up to perfection!

BETTER THAN THE TABERNACLE

The next argument for the excellency, superiority and all-sufficiency of Christ is drawn from the construction of the Tabernacle. It is introduced by:

> Now of the things which we have spoken this is the sum: We have such an high priest, who is set on the right hand of the throne of the Majesty in the heavens;
>
> A minister of the sanctuary, and of the true tabernacle, which the Lord pitched, and not man.
>
> For every high priest is ordained to offer gifts and sacrifices: wherefore it is of necessity that this man have somewhat also to offer.
>
> For if he were on earth, he should not be a priest, seeing that there are priests that offer gifts according to the law:
>
> Who serve unto the example and shadow of heavenly things, as Moses was admonished of God when he was about to make the tabernacle: for, See, saith he, that thou make all things according to the pattern shewed to thee in the mount (Heb. 8:1-5).

MOST PERFECT TYPE

The most perfect type of the Lord Jesus in the entire Bible was the Tabernacle in the wilderness. It was called the "tent of meeting," the one place where God would meet with man, and where the humanity and Deity of Christ were united in one. Every part of this building, every single little detail spoke of some characteristic of Christ and His ministry. The materials spoke of Him: The silver spoke of redemption; gold, of His Deity; wood, His humanity; brass, His judgment; the altar, His Cross; the shewbread, the Bread of Life. The candlestick spoke

of Him as the Light of the World; the golden incense pointed
to His high priestly intercession. Every detail had some message
in type which was fulfilled in Christ. This is elaborated upon
in Hebrews nine.

> For there was a tabernacle made; the first, wherein was the
> candlestick, and the table, and the shewbread; which is called
> the sanctuary.
> And after the second veil, [was] the tabernacle which is called
> the Holiest of all;
> Now when these things were thus ordained, the priests went
> always into the first tabernacle, accomplishing the service of God.
> But into the second went the high priest alone once every year,
> not without blood, which he offered for himself, and for the
> errors of the people:
> But Christ being come an high priest of good things to come,
> by a greater and more perfect tabernacle, not made with hands, that
> is to say, not of this building;
> Neither by the blood of goats and calves, but by his own blood
> he entered in once into the holy place, having obtained eternal
> redemption for us (Heb. 9:2, 3, 6, 7, 11,12).

Notice carefully the particular ministry of the high priest on
the Day of Atonement. It was to offer the blood of atonement
for the *errors* of the people. The word "error" means literally,
"sins of ignorance." Willful, premeditated sins called for judgment, as we see in Hebrews six and ten, and were already typi-
fied in the judgments under the law (Ex. 21 and 22).

Failure to avail ourselves of the ministry of the High Priest,
stubborn continuance in known and willful disobedience, must
be dealt with by our Lord. With such a provision, how can we
be excused if we neglect the means of victory: repentance, obedience to the Word, prayer and testimony? If we have failed
because we did not know His will, then surely we can find full
cleansing in His blood. But now knowing the truth, what excuse can we offer? Why not come to Him now before the de-
ceitfulness of sin dulls your senses, stifles your conviction, and
you be disapproved, to meet Him empty-handed? What has the

world to offer to those of us who have all the provisions and resources of Christ to assure us, and His promise of reward for obedience?

Well done, thou good and faithful servant (Matt. 25:21).

CHAPTER FIFTEEN

Law and Grace

And as it is appointed unto men once to die, but after this the judgment:

So Christ was once offered to bear the sins of many; and unto them that look for him shall he appear the second time without sin unto salvation (Heb. 9:27, 28).

EVERY new man is two men, the old and the new. The believer has two natures which are in continual conflict. The old nature was first, being received by our natural birth from father Adam. The new nature was last, being received by the regeneration, the new birth by the Holy Spirit. The law of nature is that the first shall hold priority and dominion over the second. It is the law of seniority. The first-born had certain rights and privileges by virtue of being the eldest. The old Adamic nature, therefore, puts up a tremendous battle for superiority over the new, described by Paul as follows:

For the flesh [the old nature] lusteth against the Spirit [the new nature], and the Spirit against the flesh: and these are contrary the one to the other (Gal. 5:17).

The old nature claims control because of being there first. But grace changes and reverses the course of nature completely, and upsets the natural order of things. By nature and birth Ishmael was first in Abraham's tent, but grace says, "In Isaac [the second] shall thy seed be called" (Gen. 21:12). By birth Esau was before Jacob in the family of Isaac, but God says, "Jacob have I loved but Esau have I hated." The elder shall serve the younger. In grace the first shall be the last, and the last shall be the first, for the elder shall serve the younger. Victory can only come when we deny the first-born of the flesh, and place the Spirit in control.

LESSON IN HEBREWS

This introduction will throw light on our study of Hebrews. These Hebrews had been saved out of legalism, and delivered from the law of ordinances and placed in the liberty of grace. But the old covenant still had its appeal and these Hebrew believers were constantly prone to slip back into legalism and compromise with their old religion. To show the folly of such a position, the author of Hebrews seeks to show the infinite superiority of Christ, as being better than the Old Testament economy of shadows, types and symbols. Christ is set forth as being of a better priesthood than that of Aaron. He was after the eternal order of Melchisedec (Heb. 7:1–17). Next He is presented as better than all the impressive solemn services of the Tabernacle, which were only a shadow of the coming One (Heb. 8:1-6). Then the superiority of Christ over the old covenant is advanced. The law made nothing perfect. A perfect law could not produce perfection. It left the best man in the world under its curse and condemnation. For over fifteen hundred years the nation of Israel was under the law of the Ten Commandments, in addition to all the ceremonial laws and ordinances, and yet after fifteen hundred years of struggling, laboring, toiling, not a single Israelite was ever saved by keeping that law. They had failed completely under the law, and after one and one-half millenniums under perfect law, they ended up by committing the capital crime of the universe, murdering the only Man who ever did keep God's law in every detail.

Jesus came, fulfilled the law, paid its penalty, bore its curse for us, and now offers salvation as a free gift of grace, without the deeds of the law. One would suppose this would be enough to cure man of ever wanting to be under the law again, but such is the perversion of human nature that he will turn to the works of self and the flesh, rather than receive God's free gift of grace. This too was the tendency of the Galatian Christians to whom Paul wrote:

> Are ye so foolish? having begun in the Spirit, are ye now made perfect by the flesh? (Gal. 3:3)

This was also the problem with the believers in Hebrews. They had been saved by grace, but were slipping back into legalism and the ceremonial and ritualistic system of types and shadows and so invited the correction of the God of grace. The old covenant of the law had failed to make men better, for the law was not given to save men or make them better but to prove man's need of grace. Of Jesus' superiority over the law it is said:

> But now hath he obtained a more excellent ministry, by how much also he is the mediator of a better covenant, which was established upon better promises.
> For if that first covenant [the law] had been faultless, then should no place have been sought for the second.
> For finding fault with them, he saith, Behold, the days come, saith the Lord, when I will make a new covenant with the house of Israel and with the house of Judah (Heb. 8:6-8).

Example of Israel

You who desire again to be under the law, consider Israel as a nation. God gave them the prophets, priests and godly kings. He committed to them the oracles of God, the covenants and a perfect law. But look at Israel now, scattered among the Gentiles, with a little handful left in the land of promise, as vassals and slaves of their conquerors. Have they been able to keep the law? Why then their sad present plight? Why the dispersion? But the day is coming when Israel will be restored in all fullness. It will not be by the law, but by the grace of God, when they confess their failure and turn to Christ. It will be the new covenant, and

> Not according to the covenant that I made with their fathers in the day when I took them by the hand to lead them out of the land of Egypt; because they continued not in my covenant, and I regarded them not, saith the Lord (Heb. 8:9).

Learn the lesson of your forefathers, ye Hebrews, and cease
your efforts to be made perfect by the law and turn to the grace
of God, and then the Lord will restore you as He will the nation
of Israel, when

> I will put my laws in their mind, and write them in their
> hearts: and I will be to them a God, and they shall be to me a
> people (Heb. 8:10).

This lesson of grace must still be repeated and repeated. How
many there are who, being saved by grace, still imagine that they
can be kept by the works of the law, instead of allowing the
"grace of God that bringeth salvation to all men" to teach them
"that denying ungodliness and worldly lusts, we should live
soberly, righteously, and godly, in this present world" (Titus
2:11, 12).

The truly victorious Christian has long ago learned to have
no confidence in the flesh, but to depend upon and surrender
all to the grace of God.

BETTER BLOOD

The next argument advanced for abandoning self, and going
on to perfection is based upon the blood of sacrifice. The new
covenant of grace is final and unalterable. It is Jesus' last will
and testament. And right here His death and the shedding of
His blood become the unbreakable seal of the security of those
who trust His finished work. The argument is introduced in
Hebrews nine:

> For where a testament is, there must also of necessity be the
> death of the testator.
> For a testament is of force after men are dead: otherwise it is
> of no strength at all while the testator liveth (Heb. 9:16, 17).

No last will or testament is binding until sealed by death,
for until death, it can still be altered, canceled or destroyed,
but once the testator is dead, his last will stands. Of this death
the shedding of blood is the evidence. From the sacrifice of
Abel throughout all the Old Testament the blood of countless
tens of thousands of animals proclaimed the truth that "the

wages of sin is death" and the price of redemption is blood. But all the blood of animals could not take away sin. And the proof of this is their continuation, and the need of being constantly repeated. For if the blood sacrifices of the law could take away sins,

> . . . then would they not have ceased to be offered? because that the worshippers once purged should have had no more conscience of sins.
> But in those sacrifices there is a remembrance again made of sins every year.
> For it is not possible that the blood of bulls and of goats should take away sins.
> But this man, after he had offered one sacrifice for sins for ever, sat down on the right hand of God;
> For by one offering he hath perfected for ever them that are sanctified (Heb. 10:2-4, 12, 14).

But when He finished the work He sealed it with His own perfect, sinless, incorruptible, precious, eternal blood, and His last will and testament now becomes effective to all who believe. Today, when a man dies, the administration of his last will and testament must be left to another. An executor or executrix is either named in the will or appointed by the court. He or she is expected to follow the prescribed instructions of the deceased in distributing his estate according to his wishes as stated in the last will. But the executor may misunderstand the desire of the deceased. The will may be contested by others, as it usually is. Many times the court finds it difficult to decide just what the testator had in mind, and why he excluded some from the will. As a result of the limitations of the administrator or lack of information, the court may distribute the estate entirely contrary to the real wish of the deceased. And nothing can be done about it, for the poor man is dead and cannot be consulted as to just what he did mean. If he could, I am sure many a dead person would rise up in righteous anger from the grave, to protest the way his estate was being handled, and his will misinterpreted and twisted. But he can't do it, and so injustice and perversion result, and too often little or nothing of the terms of the will is carried out.

The Testator Lives

But how different with the Lord Jesus. He made His will and left us His testament and covenant of grace. When He died He sealed it with His blood. But here comes the wonder. He Himself has made provision that the terms of the will shall be carried out to the letter, for He has appointed Himself as the Administrator. After sealing the will by death, making it legal and effective, He arose to become the Executor. Forty days afterward He ascended into heaven to sit on the bench as both Administrator and Judge, and He sent His special agent, the Holy Spirit, into the world with full authority to carry out the terms of His last will and testament. How wonderfully this is set forth in Hebrews 10:9,

> Then said he, Lo, I come to do thy will, O God. He taketh away the first, that he may establish the second.

This last and second testament nullifies the first. The first testament of the law is now replaced by the second testament, the last "will" of grace. Under the first all are condemned; under the last will and testament all who believe become heirs of all He possesses, heirs of God and joint-heirs with Jesus Christ.

> By the which will we are sanctified through the offering of the body of Jesus Christ once for all.
> For by one offering he hath perfected for ever them that are sanctified (Heb. 10:10, 14).

And then He sat down to administer His will:

> Whereof the Holy Ghost also is a witness to us (Heb. 10:15).

Are you a child of God? Then you should be interested in what your Lord has left you in His will. You are the beneficiary in His will. When men die here below, the heirs lose little time before they open the will to see what it contains. They can hardly wait for the necessary funeral services to end. Yet how little interest the heirs of salvation show in their inheritance. They hardly have time to read the Book of precious promises. If they only knew what it contained, they would stop everything to find out and enjoy His provisions. It will take an eternity for us to discover the wealth which He has left for us. He said:

> Father, I will that they also, whom thou hast given me, be with me where I am; that they may behold my glory, which thou hast given me (John 17:24).

We are joint-heirs with the Son of God, and the Bible is the book which tells us of our glorious future inheritance. Why then be so occupied and concerned with these temporal, fleeting things of time and matter which endure only for a moment. No wonder Paul admonishes the Colossians:

> If ye then be risen with Christ, seek those things which are above, where Christ sitteth on the right hand of God.
> Set your affection on things above, not on things on the earth.
> When Christ, who is our life, shall appear, then shall ye also appear with him in glory (Col. 3:1, 2, 4).

Oh, that God

> . . . would grant you, according to the riches of his glory, to be strengthened with might by his Spirit in the inner man;
> That Christ may dwell in your hearts by faith; that ye, being rooted and grounded in love,
> May be able to comprehend with all saints what is the breadth, and length, and depth, and height;
> And to know the love of Christ, which passeth knowledge, that ye might be filled with all the fulness of God (Eph. 3:16-19).

CHAPTER SIXTEEN

Falling from Grace

> For if we sin wilfully after that we have received the knowledge of the truth, there remaineth no more sacrifice for sins (Heb. 10:26).

WE who preach the Gospel of salvation by grace apart from the works of the law are constantly accused of preaching a gospel which gives a license to sin and *makes for loose living*. The accusation is not wholly unjustified, for we must face the fact that many who profess the grace of God are not walking worthy of their profession. To jump at the conclusion that all such are not saved would be foolish, for we know there are both carnal and spiritual believers. The Bible is full of examples of children of God who fell into sin and became a reproach to their Lord. Witness Noah, Abraham, Moses, David, Solomon, Peter and Thomas. If practical and moral sinless perfection is required to be saved, then who can stand?

But what is God going to do to those who fail and fall and come short of His perfect will? God has given two remedies. For all who will acknowledge their sin, repent, and confess it, the Lord has made provision for perfect forgiveness and cleansing. In Leviticus chapters four and five God provided a sacrifice for: Sins of Ignorance; Sins of Omission; and Sins of Defilement. In I John 1:9 we are promised:

> If we confess our sins, he is faithful and just to forgive us our sins, and to cleanse us from all unrighteousness.

But what about those believers who do not repent? Does God just overlook and forget all about it, because we are saved by grace, and when we are saved, everything is all settled forever? Or do such unrepentant ones cease to be children of God, and lose their salvation? Neither one of these ideas is taught anywhere in the Scriptures. They nowhere teach that a Christian can sin and escape the penalty. Neither do they teach that a Christian who sins is lost again. What then is the answer? Failure to face this problem squarely has given some justification to those who accuse the exponents of grace and security of preaching a dangerous gospel. Some even call it a "damnable doctrine from hell." Have we possibly given some occasion for this misunderstanding? I believe we have. To preach grace, grace, free grace, without the counterbalancing truth of the responsibilities of grace, and the penalty for the believer's sins, and suffering for our misdeeds here and now, and at the Judgment Seat of Christ, is indeed a dangerous doctrine.

GOD WILL JUDGE HIS PEOPLE

The Bible is clear that God does judge His people. To the careless child of God, He sends chastening. This may take the form of weakness, sickness and even death. If the chastening measures are ignored, God may take such an one away to be judged by fire at the Judgment Seat of Christ (I Cor. 3:14, 15). Never before has there been such a need for a clear, sound setting forth of the responsibilities of grace. The looseness and worldliness of Christians, the lethargy and indifference of professors of Christ, are the results of a one-sided, unbalanced preaching of grace, resulting in a false sense of security. Be not deceived; no Christian can indulge in known or willful sin and get away with it. While the guilt of sin is forever settled for the believer, it is nevertheless a fact that he must bear the consequences of neglect and disobedience. If I as a child of God, in a careless moment get into bad company, engage in a brawl and lose an eye in the scuffle, the Lord will forgive if I truly repent of my sin and confess it to Him, *but* I have to go through life with only one eye. He forgives, but He does not replace the eye. The scar is there to remind me ever after of the truth that I cannot be disobedient and escape the chastening. David found it out. What a price he had to pay. Here then is the revelation of the Word. When a sinner comes to Christ in true faith and receives Him as Lord and Saviour, he receives eternal life, the very life of God. But being a child of God places him under the absolute obligation of obedience to his Master. If he obeys, he is rewarded here as well as by and by. If he is disobedient, he will be forgiven if he repents and confesses, but for those who continue in known, willful disobedience, God will apply the rod. Presumptuous, continued disobedience may result in the sin unto death. This sin unto death is judged by the Lord in a variety of ways:

1. By chastening for the rest of one's life until the day of death.
2. By actual physical death (I Cor. 5:5; 11:30).
3. By being taken out of service, and becoming a castaway (I Cor. 9:27).

There are many believers who have to carry the scars of their mistakes and sins until death relieves them. The Bible is also clear that physical sickness and death result from unconfessed, known sin. But the most tragic of all are those who reach a place where God ceases to deal with them and leaves them alone until the Judgment Seat of Christ. For it is impossible to renew them again unto repentance. Like Israel, they are out of Egypt, under the blood, but die in the wilderness, before ever reaching the Canaan of victory, assurance, fruitfulness and blessing.

Hebrews Ten

The Epistle to the Hebrews contains two sections dealing with this subject of believers sinning willfully and falling short of God's best for them. The first section, Hebrews six, we have studied. The second section is Hebrews 10:26-39. These two constitute one solemn warning against "falling away" and "sinning willfully." Both are related to the sin unto death, both have to do with rewards or loss of rewards, and both point to the Judgment Seat of Christ. And between these two grave warnings the Holy Spirit gives us the only defense against the danger of incurring the chastening and judgment of God. Between Hebrews six and ten we have three chapters, seven, eight and nine, which give the most complete and exhaustive picture of Jesus Christ, our interceding High Priest in heaven. Our only assurance of not becoming guilty of the error of Hebrews six and ten is to avail ourselves of the ministry of the High Priest in heaven, by repentance and confession of our sins, and then to trust Him to "keep us from falling." There is no excuse for any believer falling into the category of castaways, since we have an adequate High Priest in heaven as set forth in chapters seven, eight, and nine of Hebrews. It is failure to avail ourselves of His ministry that causes us to fall. He is our only protection as the author of Hebrews says:

> Seeing then that we have a great high priest, that is passed into the heavens, Jesus the Son of God, let us hold fast our profession [not possession].
> For we have not an high priest which cannot be touched with the feeling of our infirmities; but was in all points tempted like as we are, yet without sin.
> Let us therefore come boldly unto the throne of grace, that we may obtain mercy [forgiveness], and find grace to help [to keep us] in time of need (Heb. 4:14-16).

We have a High Priest who is there for two reasons:

1. To forgive and cleanse when we have failed, or to obtain *mercy*.

2. To keep us from falling again, or to give "grace to help in time of need."

Now Willful Sinning

But what about those who have such an High Priest, and such an infallible Helper, and then ignore His services, refuse to avail themselves of His ministry? What about those who with all this knowledge and light, deliberately and willfully live in disobedience to Him? This is taken up in Hebrews ten. We quote at length the passage.

> For if we sin wilfully after that we have received the knowledge of the truth, there remaineth no more sacrifice for sins,
>
> But a certain fearful looking for of judgment and fiery indignation, which shall devour the adversaries.
>
> He that despised Moses' law died without mercy under two or three witnesses;
>
> Of how much sorer punishment, suppose ye, shall he be thought worthy, who hath trodden under foot the Son of God, and hath counted the blood of the covenant, wherewith he was sanctified, an unholy thing, and hath done despite unto the Spirit of grace?
>
> For we know him that hath said, Vengeance belongeth unto me, I will recompense, saith the Lord. And again, the Lord shall judge his people.
>
> It is a fearful thing to fall into the hands of the living God (Heb. 10:26-31).

What a solemn passage! It makes one tremble to contemplate the dire implications. Who is the writer talking about? The easiest way to get rid of the unpleasant message is to apply it to someone else. And this is the generally accepted interpretation. There are those who say these people were saved but through willful sinning lost their salvation again. This is the Arminian view. The Calvinistic explanation follows the same pattern as that used in explaining Hebrews 6:4-6.

WHO ARE ADDRESSED?

Before taking up who is meant by the expression, "fearful looking for of judgment and fiery indignation," we must determine who the writer is talking *to* and *about*. If we err here we shall be wrong all the way. Remember, the most common, popular and almost universally accepted view is that it refers to "professors" of Christ, who had never been born again — Hebrews who had intellectually accepted the truths about Christ, but when persecution arose, went back into Judaism because they had never been saved at all. This interpretation is in direct violation to the plain intention of the chapter.

We would refer you back to the context beginning with verse nineteen:

> Having therefore, brethren, boldness to enter into the holiest by the blood of Jesus,
>
> By a new and living way, which he hath consecrated for us, through the veil, that is to say, his flesh (Heb. 10:19, 20).

Every Bible student is agreed that these words are addressed to and refer to "born-again believers." They are called "brethren," who have access unto the holiest by the new and living way. They are believers. There is no argument here.

> And having an high priest over the house of God;
>
> Let us draw near with a true heart in full assurance of faith, having our hearts sprinkled from an evil conscience, and our bodies washed with pure water (Heb. 10:21, 22).

Again there is no disagreement in interpreting this passage. All are agreed that only born-again believers have an High Priest over the House of God, and only believers are invited to draw near in full assurance. No argument here! We go on.

> Let us hold fast the profession of our faith without wavering; (for he is faithful that promised;)
>
> And let us consider one another to provoke unto love and to good works:
>
> Not forsaking the assembling of ourselves together, as the manner of some is; but exhorting one another: and so much the more, as ye see the day approaching (Heb. 10:23-25).

No one will deny these words are addressed to believers. They are admonished to "hold fast their profession." If they were not saved, they would be making a false profession and certainly a hypocrite would not be encouraged to hold fast his "false" profession. Furthermore, they are admonished to good works, to attend the assembly of the saints, to exhort one another in view of the coming of Christ.

Up until now I have heard no objection. All agree that this applies only to genuinely, thoroughly converted and truly born-again believers. But now comes the shock in the next verse:

> For if we sin wilfully after that we have received the knowledge of the truth, there remaineth no more sacrifice for sins,
> But a certain fearful looking for of judgment (Heb. 10:26, 27).

Please notice there is no break in the line of reasoning. It is still speaking of born-again believers and continues without break, "For if we sin wilfully." By what rule of Bible interpretation, reason or logic can we make this refer to unsaved people, as is done by many scholars and teachers, and dutifully followed and repeated by the students? What right has anyone to say that Hebrews 10:19-25 applies to believers and then suddenly at the following verse that it is to be applied to Hebrew professors who are not possessors? The writer includes himself and says, "For if *we* sin wilfully after that *we* have received the knowledge of the truth . . . ." Whatever our interpretation of the balance of the passage may be, we may be sure it deals with God's children and constitutes a solemn warning against willful, presumptuous sinning against better light and in the face of clear warning and admonition.

Before rejecting the clear language of the text, re-examine the subject with an open mind. It is exceedingly difficult to abandon traditional interpretations, but our search for truth should never become static, but should go on from strength to strength, for:

> . . . the path of the just is as the shining light, that shineth more and more unto the perfect day (Prov. 4:18).

Prayerfully re-study the subject of how God deals with the sins of the saints. I repeat, the great truth of a loving God who does chasten His children, and the greatly needed preaching of the coming Judgment Seat of Christ is the truth which balances the preaching of free grace, and is the answer to the question:

Shall we sin that grace may abound? God forbid, for how shall we that are dead to sin live any longer therein?

Remember, the Bible says, "The Lord shall judge his people." It will not be a judgment of condemnation, but a judgment of correction and receiving of rewards.

CHAPTER SEVENTEEN

God Will Judge His People

> It is a fearful thing to fall into the hands of the living God (Heb. 10:31).

THIS verse must be viewed in its context. Before deciding for *whom* it will be a fearful thing to fall into the hands of a living God, we must read what precedes the verse. It is not a fearful thing for everyone, but only for a certain class. They are described in Hebrews 10:26-39.

> For if we sin wilfully after that we have received the knowledge of the truth, there remaineth no more sacrifice for sins (Heb. 10:26).

We are dealing with Christians who deliberately continue in a life of willful, presumptuous disobedience to God. It says definitely "if we," by which the writer of Hebrews includes himself. It is a sin against better light, for it is willful sin *after we have received the knowledge of the truth.* It is not dealing with sins of ignorance, or sins of omission or defilement. He is not referring to the case of a believer being "overtaken in a fault" (Gal. 6:1), or yielding to fear or the flesh in a moment of weakness, like Peter (Matt. 26:70). It is instead, deliberate, willful, presumptuous sin against better light, like the sin of Ananias and Sapphira (Acts 5), and the sin of Nadab and Abihu (Lev. 10). It is the "sin unto death."

No More Sacrifice

For those who continue in known sin

> . . . there remaineth no more sacrifice for sins, But a certain fearful looking for of judgment and fiery indignation, which shall devour the adversaries (Heb. 10:26, 27).

140

The Lord stands ready to forgive and cleanse His child upon repentance and confession, but if he allows sin to remain unconfessed, God may step in and chasten such an one by the judgment of sickness and weakness (I Cor. 11:30) or even death. He must pay the penalty. This judgment is called a fiery indignation, but by this very judgment and fiery indignation the adversary who abetted our temptation and stubborn disobedience is destroyed and his work brought to nought. Instead of giving up His child to the adversary the devil, the Lord chastens His child, and thus robs the adversary of his victim. The judgment and fiery indignation of Hebrews 10:27 does not destroy the impenitent prodigal, but it destroys the adversary's plan, while it corrects the erring one.

The Old Testament Example

To illustrate this truth, reference is made to God's provision for just such a case under the law of Moses. He says:

> He that despised Moses' law died without mercy under two or three witnesses (Heb. 10:28).

This statement furnishes the key to our passage. We are referred to the law of Moses which clearly and unmistakably made known God's will concerning certain sins: idolatry, profanity, Sabbath-breaking, disrespect of parents, murder, stealing, lying and adultery. These things were strictly forbidden and no Israelite had any excuse if he committed them. For deliberate, presumptuous transgression of these clearly forbidden sins there was no sacrifice provided, but death was the penalty.

The high priest could intercede for any Israelite who committed certain sins. These were of three kinds mentioned in Leviticus chapters four and five. In Leviticus chapters one and two we have God's provision for the sinner in the Burnt Offering and the Meal Offering, representing the death and resurrection of Christ, and resulting in the third offering, the Peace Offering. The last two of the five offerings in Leviticus chapters four and five are the Sin Offering and the Trespass Offer-

ing. These offerings were for the cleansing and forgiveness of
sins committed by the children of Israel. There are three classes
of sins dealt with, and they are classified as:

1. Sins of Ignorance.
2. Sins of Omission.
3. Sins of Defilement.

For any of these sins a complete provision was made in the
Sin and Trespass Offerings.

Sins of Ignorance

If a soul shall sin through ignorance against any of the commandments of the LORD concerning things which ought not to be
done, and shall do against any of them:

And if the whole congregation of Israel sin through ignorance,
and the thing be hid from the eyes of the assembly . . . and are
guilty;

When the sin, which they have sinned against it, is known,
then the congregation shall offer a young bullock for the sin, and
bring him before the tabernacle of the congregation.

And the elders of the congregation shall lay their hands upon
the head of the bullock before the LORD: and the bullock shall
be killed before the LORD.

And the priest shall dip his finger in some of the blood . . . .
. . . and the priest shall make an atonement for them, and it
shall be forgiven them (Lev. 4:2, 13-15, 17, 20).

God had made full provision for sins committed because they
did not fully know God's will.

Sins of Omission

The second provision was for sins of omission.

And if a soul sin, and hear the voice of swearing, and is a
witness, whether he hath seen or known of it; if he do not utter
it, then he shall bear his iniquity (Lev. 5:1).

The third sin was the sin of defilement.

Or if a soul touch any unclean thing . . . and if it be hidden
from him; he also shall be unclean, and guilty (Lev. 5:2).

For these sins provision was made:

> And it shall be, when he shall be guilty in one of these things,
> that he shall confess that he hath sinned in that thing:
> And he shall bring his tresspass-offering unto the LORD for his sin
> . . . and the priest shall make an atonement for him concerning
> his sin (Lev. 5:5, 6).

The Lord has graciously made forgiveness possible for the weaknesses of His children, their mistakes and errors, for their sins of ignorance, sins of omission and defilement. But for the Israelite who deliberately and presumptuously committed sin against the plain revelation of the Lord and continued therein, there was no offering provided. Nowhere in the law was "willful" sin left unpunished. A few Scriptures will make this clear.

> But if a man come presumptuously upon his neighbour, to slay
> him with guile; thou shalt take him from mine altar, that he
> may die (Ex. 21:14).

Notice carefully the wording of this sin. It is a presumptuous sin, committed willfully and deliberately with full knowledge and warning of its consequences, and God says, "Take him from mine altar." The sacrifice on the altar cannot prevent such an one from paying the penalty. The same penalty applied to other presumptuous sins which had plainly been forbidden, such as smiting one's father or mother, theft, adultery, etc.

This is the law which the writer of Hebrews refers to when he says:

> He that despised Moses' law died without mercy under two or
> three witnesses (Heb. 10:28).

And then he applies this to the matter of sinning willfully —not under the law but under grace— and continues:

> Of how much sorer punishment, suppose ye, shall he be thought
> worthy, who hath trodden under foot the Son of God, and hath
> counted the blood of the covenant, wherewith he was sanctified,
> an unholy thing, and hath done despite unto the Spirit of grace?
> (Heb. 10:29).

Who Are They?

Again the all-important question is, Who are these mentioned as treading underfoot the Son of God, and counting the blood of the covenant an unholy thing and having done despite to the Spirit of grace? It is an important question, for either they were unsaved or saved. It must be one or the other. They are said to be "sanctified with the blood of Christ." Can it be said by any stretch of the imagination that an unconverted sinner has been sanctified by the blood of Christ? But there is more, for verse thirty continues:

> For we know him that hath said, Vengeance belongeth unto me, I will recompense, saith the Lord. And again, The Lord shall judge his people.
> It is a fearful thing to fall into the hands of the living God (Heb. 10:30, 31).

There is no escaping the words, "The Lord shall judge his people." This is a judgment for willful, deliberate, continued disobedience until God must step in, according to His word and purpose that He will judge *His people*.

The Final Proof

But the final argument is in the closing verse of this chapter. Notice carefully the descriptive words. In warning the believer against this danger of becoming a castaway, the writer gives this wise counsel:

> But call to remembrance the former days, in which, after ye were illuminated, ye endured a great fight of afflictions;
> Partly, whilst ye were made a gazingstock both by reproaches and afflictions; and partly, whilst ye became companions of them that were so used (Heb. 10:32, 33).

Here we have the evidence of a true work of grace, the fruits of a real salvation. They had been illuminated; they suffered for their testimony, and even became a gazingstock by reproaches. But there is much more.

> For ye had compassion of me in my bonds, and took joyfully the spoiling of your goods, knowing in yourselves that ye have in heaven a better and an enduring substance (Heb. 10:34).

Is this a description of an unconverted person? Think of it. These folks were not only saved, but were laden with fruit, as the evidence of it. They had compassion on the writer in his bonds, took *joyfully* the spoiling of their goods, and to crown it all, they had the *assurance of* salvation, for of them it is said:

> Knowing . . . that ye have in heaven a better and an enduring substance.

Matter of Assurance

But let us go on, and see the evidence mounting. Listen to this admonition:

> Cast not away therefore your confidence, which hath great recompence of reward (Heb. 10:35).

Two words are of tremendous importance. They are *confidence* and *reward*. It does not read, "cast not away therefore your *salvation*." It is not a matter of losing salvation, but losing the *assurance*. And the danger is losing the *reward*. But the evidence mounts still more:

> For ye have need of patience, that, after ye have done the will of God, ye might receive the promise [reward] (Heb. 10:36).

The reward will be given at the Judgment Seat of Christ, when Jesus comes. There the work of God's children will be judged. There faithfulness will be rewarded. The unrepentant disobedient will be dealt with and the castaways shall be saved so as by fire. One passage alone will determine this. Consider again the words of I Corinthians 3:12-15:

> Now if any man build upon this foundation [that determines salvation] gold, silver, precious stones, wood, hay, stubble;
> Every man's work shall be made manifest: for the day shall declare it, because it shall be revealed by fire; and the fire shall try every man's work of what sort it is.
> If any man's work abide which he hath built thereupon, he shall receive a reward.

> If any man's work shall be burned, he shall suffer loss: but
> he himself shall be saved; yet so as by fire.

It is in view of this Judgment Seat of Christ that the admonition in Hebrews ten is given. It is a reminder that a reckoning
is coming.

> For yet a little while, and he that shall come will come, and
> will not tarry (Heb. 10:37).

We are to evaluate everything in the light of Christ's coming.
Then nothing else will count, and hence the closing warning:

> Now the just shall live by faith: but if any man draw back,
> my soul shall have no pleasure in him (Heb. 10:38).

The warning is against drawing back, instead of pressing
on for the crown. This is the impact of the opening warning:

> . . . if we sin wilfully after that we have received the knowl-
> edge of the truth . . . (Heb. 10:26a).

This is "drawing back." Now what is involved in drawing
back? Does it mean such an one is lost? Or does it refer to the
loss of rewards, and "suffering loss" at Jesus' coming? The answer is in the final verse. The writer, fearing that some might
misinterpret the meaning of "drawing back," hastens to explain:

> But we are not of them who draw back unto perdition; but of
> them that believe to the saving of the soul (Heb. 10:39).

Here is the final answer. Do not suppose that the believer
can draw back unto perdition. He can draw back and invite the
judgment of God in sickness, weakness and chastening and
even commit the sin unto death, but God cannot go back on His
promise, and so we are reminded that "we are not of them
that draw back unto perdition; but of them that believe to the
saving of the soul." Yes, it is possible to draw back, *but not
unto perdition.*

Shall we then sin that grace may abound? Because we are
saved by grace, can we then live as we please? Does the Gospel
of the grace of God give us license to sin? Don't be deceived!

> God is not mocked: for whatsoever a man soweth, that shall he also reap (Gal. 6:7).

When a person receives Jesus Christ as Saviour, the guilt of sin is removed forever, past, present and future. There is no condemnation for the believer. He has passed from death unto life (John 5:24). But it is possible to neglect this salvation (Heb. 2:3). He may come short of God's best for him (Heb. 4:1). Well may we be reminded, that just because our salvation is free and unearned, our responsibility to "work it out" is all the greater. There will be an accounting, and in the light of this clear revelation let us heed the warning of Colossians 3:23-25:

> And whatsoever ye do, do it heartily, as to the Lord, and not unto men;
>
> Knowing that of the Lord ye shall receive the reward of the inheritance: for ye serve the Lord Christ.
>
> But he that doeth wrong shall receive for the wrong which he hath done: and there is no respect of persons.

CHAPTER EIGHTEEN

The Triumph of Faith

THE eleventh chapter of Hebrews has been called the "faith" chapter of the Bible, recording for us a long register of heroes of the Old Testament who were victorious and who,

> . . . through faith subdued kingdoms, wrought righteousness, obtained promises, stopped the mouths of lions,
>
> Quenched the violence of fire, escaped the edge of the sword, out of weakness were made strong, waxed valiant in fight, turned to flight the armies of the aliens (Heb. 11:33, 34).

It is more than a chapter on faith, for it records the "victories" of faith. Following as it does the tenth chapter of Hebrews, it is of tremendous significance. The theme of Hebrews must not be lost sight of. It is a solemn warning against coming short of victory, an appeal to believers not to neglect their so great salvation, but to press on in spite of all difficulties. The danger of letting our opportunities of grace slip (2:1), of coming short of victory (4:1), of remaining spiritual babes (5:12) is constantly held before us, and the terrible consequences of disobedience are stated again and again. A Christian can go so far in refusing the correction of the Lord that finally he comes to a place of "hardening," from where it is impossible to bring him again to repentance. Willful sinning, deliberate, continued disobedience and failure to judge known sin in our lives may result in our "falling away." This results in God's judgment with only one purpose in mind, that of correction, and never of damnation. If it were a matter of salvation, God would not seek to correct them by dealing so severely with them, for the Lord does not chasten the sinner. As we shall see in chapter twelve, "whom the Lord loveth he chasteneth."

Who Is Sufficient?

The implications are such that many might reply, If God deals so with His children, who then can gain the victory? Is there anyone who can attain and receive the commendation of the Lord? These questions are answered in chapter eleven. Yes, indeed, victory is possible if we will but heed the warning, and hold fast the "beginning of our confidence firm unto the end." Hebrews eleven gives a register of some examples to encourage us. Among others he names Abel, Enoch, Noah, Abraham, Sara, Isaac, Jacob, Joseph, Moses, Rahab, Gideon, Barak, Jephthae, David, Samuel and the prophets. These all were men and women of like passion as we are, and yet they gained the victory.

Not Perfect Men

None of these were perfect or devoid of temptation. With far less light than we have today, they pressed on in spite of temporary defeats, frequent stumbling and setbacks, and unspeakable oppositions. But victory implies a battle, for there can be no victory where there is no fighting. Salvation is free, but victory means sacrifice; to win the race means discipline. We shall see the price of victory in some of these examples, but before we do, we must first look at the nature of the faith which made the victory possible. This chapter divides itself easily into four distinct divisions:

1. The definition of faith (vv. 1-3).
2. The examples of faith (vv. 4-32).
3. The price of the victory of faith (vv. 33-38).
4. The reward of victorious faith (vv. 39, 40).

The Definition of Faith

Now faith is the substance of things hoped for, the evidence of things not seen.

For by it the elders obtained a good report.

> Through faith we understand that the worlds were framed
> by the word of God, so that things which are seen were not made
> of things which do appear (Heb. 11:1-3).

This is God's own definition of a conquering faith. It is interesting to note that the definition as given by Webster closely follows God's own definition. The dictionary defines faith as

> The assent of the mind to the truth of divine revelation, on the
> authority of God's testimony, accompanied by a cordial assent of
> the will or approbation of the heart; and entire confidence or trust
> in God's character and declarations, and in the character and
> doctrines of Christ, with an unreserved surrender of the will to
> His guidance, and dependence on His merits for salvation, also
> called evangelical, justifying or saving faith.

The first thing we find then, about faith, is that it is an assent to, and an acceptance of truth, simply upon the word of someone else, without proof or any other evidence. It is believing what I cannot see, hear, feel, taste, smell or understand. Faith is accepting the word of another just because we believe what he says is true. It, therefore, comes down to this simple fact, that faith is confidence in another. This is the general nature of simple faith. To this the writer of Hebrews agrees. He says:

> Now faith is the substance of things hoped for, the evidence
> of things not seen (Heb. 11:1).

Faith is believing the unreasonable, the impossible and the unexplainable, because someone else, in whom we have absolute confidence has said it was so, and upon his word we believe it, without asking any further proof.

THE SOURCE OF AUTHORITY

That brings us to the next fact about faith, the authority of the one in whom we place our confidence. We do not just believe anything that anyone says. Our faith in an individual's word rests upon a number of factors. First, it rests upon the reliability and record of the one who says it. If the one whom we are asked to believe is one who has a reputation for dishonesty and has been proven unreliable before, we refuse to put our faith in him. If on the other hand he has a record of long years of reliability and dependability, then we dare to entrust him with our faith.

THE AUTHOR OF OUR FAITH

In the same way Bible faith, true saving faith, is gained through believing the Word of another, wholly independent of any other proof. The Scriptures teach us that we are saved by faith in God's Word. We believe men's word if they have proven they are reliable. Just so, God asks we shall believe *Him* on the record of His Word, backed up by an eternity of faithfulness, wherein no one who has ever put his trust in Him has ever been lost or disappointed. John tells us in I John 5:9, 10:

> If we receive the witness of men, the witness of God is greater: for this is the witness of God which he hath testified of his Son.
> He that believeth on the Son of God hath the witness in himself: he that believeth not God hath made him a liar; because he believeth not the record that God gave of his Son.

Please notice that last phrase, *because he believeth not the record that God gave of his Son.* God asks you, if you want to be saved, to believe what He has to say about His Son, Jesus Christ. As an illustration of Bible faith the writer of Hebrews refers to the record of creation.

> Through faith we understand that the worlds were framed by the word of God (Heb. 11:3).

The natural man wants to reason out the origin of the universe, and comes up with a thousand speculations, none of which satisfy, for theory after theory of man is discarded almost before it is stated. But the believer rests upon the simple statement of God.

> In the beginning God created the heaven and the earth (Gen. 1:1).

There it is. Take it or leave it. There will never be a better answer given. It is absolute, final and true. God does not stop to explain; He is not obliged to satisfy our curiosity or stoop to satisfy man's credulity. Faith comes to rest in the first verse of the Bible, and infidelity begins right here.

The Key to Faith

This first verse of Genesis then, is the first example of faith. If you can believe Genesis 1:1 that God always was (you can't understand that), and that He made the whole universe out of nothing by just speaking a word, I say, if you can believe that, then you can believe anything else this God says. Then you can believe the whole Bible, believe all the miracles, believe that God could become man, that He could be both God and man, that He could die for the whole world, that His blood can cleanse your sin. Then you can believe that you are a sinner, because God says it, and that you cannot be saved except by believing on and receiving His Son, Jesus Christ.

Examples of Faith

Having given the definition of faith, the recorder of Hebrews now proceeds to demonstrate the power of faith, not only to save but to give victory. This is the burden of Hebrews, in order that these babes in Christ might grow up into spiritual manhood. He refers to some sixteen Old Testament saints by name, and a number of others by inference. They were all men and women with the same faults and weaknesses common to us. They stumbled and fell, but did not remain down. They repented and began again until finally they conquered. The one common experience of all of them, however, was this: The victory did not come the easy way, but in every case involved a sacrifice of self. Abel's victory cost him his life. Enoch's victory cost him the plaudits of the world as he walked alone with God in a desperately evil age. Noah's victory cost him disappointment, for after all his preaching, only seven others entered the ark. Abraham's victory of faith cost him the sacrifice of Isaac, whom God demanded but graciously spared. The victory of Isaac's faith was surrendering his will and desire to favor his pet son, Esau, and give to Jacob, who deceived him, the blessing he intended for Esau. Jacob's victory came at the price of paralysis. He wrestled at Peniel and came out a victor but a cripple for life. Joseph gained the victory by being despised by his brethren. Moses paid the price of victory by renouncing his claim to the wealth of Egypt. And so we might go on with all the rest of the list of heroes.

Our Examples

Everyone of these was saved by simple faith, but the victory of faith was only won through sacrifice. To follow Jesus means Gethsemane and Calvary, but it leads finally to resurrection glory and reward. Does the price seem too high and have you lagged behind, fearing the reproach of discipleship and the price of uncompromising separation? To every believer comes the invitation, "Take my yoke upon you, and learn of me." It is to believers that Paul writes in Romans twelve:

> I beseech you therefore, brethren, by the mercies of God, that ye present your bodies a living sacrifice, holy, acceptable unto God, which is your reasonable service.
>
> And be not conformed to this world: but be ye transformed by the renewing of your mind, that ye may prove what is that good, and acceptable, and perfect, will of God (Rom. 12:1, 2).

Be not deceived, victory means a battle, wounds and scars, disappointments and sacrifice, but in the end the glorious crown of victory. Notice the description of what it cost these heroes of the faith. They were

> . . . tortured, not accepting deliverance; that they might obtain a better resurrection:
>
> And others had trial of cruel mockings and scourgings, yea, moreover of bonds and imprisonment:
>
> They were stoned, they were sawn asunder, were tempted, were slain with the sword: they wandered about in sheepskins and goatskins; being destitute, afflicted, tormented;

(Of whom the world was not worthy:) they wandered in deserts, and in mountains, and in dens and caves of the earth (Heb. 11:35-38).

God has not yet asked us to make such sacrifices as these. He has graciously spared us most of these things, and then we complain when He asks us to surrender our bodies to His service, separate ourselves from the world, abstain from sinful pleasures, refuse to compromise with evil. He asks us to witness for Him, without being stoned for our witness. He asks us to study His Word, without being imprisoned for it. He asks us "not to forsake the assembling of ourselves together" without having the meeting broken up by the gestapo. And then we complain and refuse to yield our all to Him. Oh, shame on us for our unwillingness to make such small sacrifices for Him. Instead of heeding the admonition, "be not conformed to this world" (Rom. 12:2), we are afraid of being called odd or fanatical, and so we just go along with the world in its pleasures and amusements. Oh, if we could visualize what we are losing in the end for not daring to stand without fear or compromise for Christ! May God forgive us and help us to keep our eyes on the One who suffered on the Cross, for the joy of saving us.

> Let this mind be in you, which was also in Christ Jesus:
>
> Who, being in the form of God, thought it not robbery to be equal with God:
>
> But made himself of no reputation, and took upon him the form of a servant, and was made in the likeness of men:
>
> And being found in fashion as a man, he humbled himself, and became obedient unto death, even the death of the cross (Phil. 2:5-8).

CHAPTER NINETEEN
The Rewards of Faith

THE word "faith" occurs twenty-one times in Hebrews eleven. The expression "through faith" occurs five times, and the expression "by faith" is used thirteen times. It is the record of the overcoming, victorious faith of the heroes of the Old Testament. These heroes had more than simple saving faith by which they believed unto salvation. In addition they had faith which resulted in sacrifice, separation and service. It was a faith which did not stand still but "went on to perfection." It was a growing, developing, increasing faith which resulted in victory at any cost. We must distinguish between saving faith and obedient faith. Thousands of believers have trusted Christ for their salvation, but are not obeying Him in service. It is a strange paradox that Christians will trust God for their souls' eternal salvation, but dare not trust Him with their bodily needs. They have committed their eternal destiny into His hands by faith, but fail to yield and surrender their temporal things to Him, and trust Him for the things of this life. They are anxious and fearful, and worry about their temporal supply, their health, business and possessions, instead of trusting Him for these just as implicitly as they have trusted Him for eternal life.

LITTLE FAITH

There is a "little" faith, which fails to give perfect peace, and there is a "great" faith which claims the victory. Jesus rebuked His disciples for their "little" faith, but commended a poor, outcast Gentile mother for her "great" faith. In Matthew six Jesus said:

155

> . . . Take no thought for your life, what ye shall eat, or what
> ye shall drink; nor yet for your body, what ye shall put on. Is
> not the life more than meat, and the body than raiment?
> . . . Consider the lilies of the field, how they grow; they toil
> not, neither do they spin:
> And yet I say unto you, That even Solomon in all his glory
> was not arrayed like one of these.
> Wherefore, if God so clothe the grass of the field, which to day
> is, and to morrow is cast into the oven, shall he not much more
> clothe you, O ye of LITTLE FAITH? (Matt. 6:25, 28-30)

These words were spoken to His own disciples. But listen to
Jesus as He speaks to the Syrophenician woman. She was a
Gentile. She had no legal claim to Messiah's attention. She
knew this, and realized the truth of Jesus' words,

> It is not meet to take the children's bread, and cast it to dogs
> (Matt. 15:26).

One would think that this stern rebuke would have discouraged her on the spot. Jesus calls her a "dog" who had no right
or claim to the children's bread. But instead of being offended,
she said:

> . . . Truth, Lord: yet the dogs eat of the crumbs which fall
> from their masters' table (Matt. 15:27).

It was a faith which would not be discouraged or denied, a
faith which could not be insulted. She was willing to take the
humblest place, make any sacrifice to win His favor. And Jesus
rewarded her and said:

> . . . O woman, great is thy faith: be it unto thee even as thou
> wilt (Matt. 15:28).

What kind of faith is yours? Is it just faith enough for salvation, faith to keep you out of hell, and take you to heaven when
you die? That is "little" faith. Or has your faith grown and developed till it seeks to remove mountains and work for something "better" than mere salvation. The heroes of the faith
in Hebrews eleven had great faith, for they were not satisfied
by being merely saved, but were willing to pay any price for
something *plus* salvation. By this overcoming faith,

> Women received their dead raised to life again: and others
> were tortured, not accepting deliverance; that they might obtain
> a better resurrection (Heb. 11:35).

It was something over and above just sharing in the resurrection of the saved. It was a better part in this resurrection.

How is this faith obtained? How may we receive a conquering victorious faith which lifts us above all the circumstances of life? It is not a new faith, but a development of "little" faith into "great" faith. It is a development, a growing up in grace and knowledge of Jesus Christ. We have seen in chapter five that the Hebrew Christians were people of "little" faith, babes in Christ, still nursing on milk. They are admonished to go on till they can take solid food. "Let us go on to maturity" is the admonition. The secret is suggested in the words of Jesus quoted from Matthew 6:28,

> Consider the lilies of the field, how they grow.

Jesus calls attention to *how* they grow. By appropriating God's good gifts of sunshine and rain they just simply grow. In the same way we must grow in our faith. There are three principle stages of this growth suggested by the first three heroes of the faith mentioned in Hebrews eleven. It is significant that three, and only three men who lived before the flood, are included in the category of faith. They are Abel, Enoch and Noah. All the others lived *after* the judgment of the Deluge. These three men illustrate the three steps or stages in the growth of faith. They are in their order:

1. Abel — Worshiping by faith.
2. Enoch — Walking by faith.
3. Noah — Working by faith.

Abel worshiped God at the appointed altar. It was a picture of Christ as the Lamb of God, dying upon the altar of the Cross. Here all faith must begin. The next man mentioned is Enoch, who walked with God for three hundred years. In addition to the worship of Abel, and as a result of it, we now walk and fellowship with God, living a life of separation with God, and prove to the world that it is possible to walk with God in the most wicked age of the world's history. And then the last of the antediluvian heroes is a man who "worked" for God. He was Noah who built the Ark, and who put his faith in action.

SAME ORDER IN PENTATEUCH

We have the same order followed in the first five books of the Bible. The first book, Genesis, is the record of the fall, and the entrance of death by sin. Exodus is the book of redemption by the blood of the Passover Lamb. But the record does not end there with a redeemed people out of Egypt. Their goal is the land of victory in Canaan. And so we have three more books of Moses which may be called the books of:

1. Leviticus — Worship.
2. Numbers — Walk.
3. Deuteronomy — Work.

The book following Exodus (the book of redemption) is Leviticus, with its laws and regulations for the sacrifices, service and worship in the Tabernacle. This is followed by Numbers, which is the record of Israel's walking in the wilderness. And then follows Deuteronomy which, as the name indicates, is the book of the law, and speaks of works and full obedience to God's commands. This is the path of victory. Until we have learned to worship, we shall never be able to walk, much less to work acceptably for God. This order cannot be violated. God is more interested in our worship than in our work, for He knows that unless we first worship, our work will be only in the energy of the flesh. Before we can begin to walk and work, we must stop at headquarters to receive our orders and equipment for the journey and the task. The reason so much Christian work and activity accomplishes little or nothing is because it is not preceded by worship, quiet study of the Word and time for prayer. Before Martha's service can be its best, she must first take Mary's place. Abel precedes Enoch, and Enoch precedes Noah.

Does your service for Christ seem fruitless and discouraging? Then ask yourself, How much time have I spent in worship, in getting orders from the Word, in seeking guidance by prayer? We can be so busy in ceaseless religious activities that we become powerless from lack of worship. How much time have you spent today in worship? When we see the programs of many churches, with two pages of the church bulletin filled with announcements of activities, meetings, clubs, societies, committees and plans for baseball games and church sales and suppers, and yet see so little spiritual fruit and results, it is safe to say that the prayer meeting is the poorest attended meeting of the week, and precious little time is left for worship. The Lord not only seeks workers for the harvest, but seeks also those to worship Him (John 4:23).

THEN WALK

The rest comes naturally and should be easy. If your prayer life, your communion is healthy and strong, it will be reflected in your walk. The people in Acts four, when they saw the boldness of Peter and John

> . . . marvelled; and they took knowledge [notice] of them, that they had been with Jesus (Acts 4:13).

Our walk too will reflect the time we have spent at Jesus' feet. Our testimony will mean little unless our walk is above reproach. And then work will follow. Until we have worshiped and our walk in itself is a testimony, our work will avail but little.

THE GREAT PERSPECTIVE

All this is suggested in the record of the heroes of the faith in Hebrews eleven and wonderfully illustrated in worshiping Abel, walking Enoch and working Noah. But it was not without a sacrifice. Many were the obstacles in their way. Abel had to face the hatred of his brother Cain. Enoch had to separate himself from the world in his walking with God. Noah had to face the jeering and scoffing of the crowd while he built the Ark on dry ground, and preached of coming judgment.

The secret of it all, however, was a matter of perspective. They looked beyond the immediate and the present. They translated all their trials into terms of the future; they weighed all their sacrifices in the balances of eternity. They had their eyes on the reward. They were not satisfied with "little" faith, but strove for a conquering faith. They, like Paul, counted all things but loss for the prize at the end of the race. It is mentioned over and over again. Notice verse six:

> . . . he that cometh to God must believe that he is, and that he is a rewarder of them that diligently seek him (Heb. 11:6).

Of Abraham it is said that when God called him, he obeyed and went, not knowing whither God was leading him,

> For he looked for a city which hath foundations, whose builder and maker is God (Heb. 11:10).

These overcomers saw the rewards afar off, and

> . . . were persuaded of them, and embraced them, and confessed that they were strangers and pilgrims on the earth.
>
> For they that say such things declare plainly that they seek a country (Heb. 11:13, 14).

Again and again in this chapter we are reminded of the secret of victory in keeping our eyes fixed upon the future glory. When these conquerors were tortured and tried and threatened with death, they refused deliverance

> . . . that they might obtain a better resurrection (Heb. 11:35).

What is meant by a better resurrection? Every believer will be present at the first resurrection of the saved at Jesus' coming for His own, but all believers will not "obtain a better resurrection." Only the overcomers will share in this, for we cannot receive an overcomer's crown without overcoming. At the resurrection and the Judgment Seat of Christ, the rewards will be distributed on the basis of our present faithfulness. Some will be ashamed at His coming; some will be saved "so as by fire," some will fail to receive a full reward, while others will obtain a "better resurrection." It may be translated, "something additional and better at the resurrection."

If these Old Testament heroes with the limited light and opportunities were able to overcome, then what excuse can we give with all the added light which we possess, when we meet Jesus? For we have much more promised than they. The chapter closes with a reminder of this. It climaxes the whole argument.

> And these all, having obtained a good report through faith, received not the promise:
> God having provided some better thing for us, that they without us should not be made perfect (Heb. 11:39, 40).

These saints did not receive their rewards when they died and went to the place of the saved. They must wait until we also appear for our rewards. God has something better for us. We are members of the Body of Christ. We shall, if we are faithful, reign over the earth. Paul says to Timothy:

> If we suffer, we shall also reign with him (II Tim. 2:12).

And these Old Testament overcomers must, therefore, wait until that day when Jesus comes to be glorified in His saints,

> . . . that they without us should not be made perfect [complete] (Heb. 11:40b).

Our faith determines our salvation; our faithfulness determines our rewards. And the secret — worshiping, walking, working, with our eyes on Jesus, so,

> . . . let us run with patience the race that is set before us.
> Looking unto Jesus the author and finisher of our faith (Heb. 12:1, 2).

CHAPTER TWENTY

You Are Being Watched

THE Bible presents the Christian life under a wide range of figures, all of them suggestive and descriptive of the believer's experience. He is compared to a child, a sheep, a house, a temple, a farm, a pilgrim, a soldier, a bride, members of a body, and many other things. One of the most colorful is that of an athlete, running in a race to obtain the prize or trophy. Such is the figure with which Hebrews twelve opens:

> Wherefore seeing we also are compassed about with so great a cloud of witnesses, let us lay aside every weight, and the sin which doth so easily beset us, and let us run with patience the race that is set before us (Heb. 12:1).

The figure is taken from a race track in a great arena, with a multitude of rooters and fans in the seats of the giant amphitheater. They are described as a great cloud of witnesses or spectators. In the stands, tier upon tier sit the eager onlookers witnessing the event with great interest. Below is the race track where the athletes are running, with but one goal in mind, not only to finish the course but to win the coveted prize. To the Hebrews of the dispersion this figure would be familiar, for racing was the popular sport of that day.

THE WITNESSES

In this picture of the race track there are three things with which the chapter occupies itself. They are the spectators, the contestants and the prize the runners receive as they cross the goal line. The runners in this race are believers who have qualified for the race by being "born again" through faith in

Jesus Christ. These runners are not trying to reach heaven by their efforts. They are already saved and sure of heaven. We are not running or working for our salvation. We are saved by grace "without the works of the law." To earn salvation we cannot lift a finger or move a foot. Many people imagine that the Christian life is running a race to get to heaven, and that they may eventually run out of wind and fail to reach the goal before they get their second wind. I listened to an earnest but poorly instructed preacher once who addressed his congregation as follows: "I am preaching today on a text of only four words, taken from the first epistle of Paul to the Corinthians, chapter nine, verse twenty-six. The text is, 'I therefore so run.' There are three points to my sermon. The first point is, you've got to run to get to heaven. Second, you've got to run awful fast to get to heaven; and third, you've got to keep right on running to get to heaven."

With great enthusiasm he urged his shouting congregation to keep on running fast lest they be too late. He had them running, jumping, digging, diving, climbing and flying in their efforts to get to heaven.

No Other Way

What a pity he did not know that there is only one way to get to heaven, and he that

> . . . climbeth up some other way, the same is a thief and a robber (John 10:1).

I was tempted to write my preacher friend a letter asking him to read carefully Romans 9:16,

> So then it is not of him that willeth, nor of him that runneth, but of God that sheweth mercy.

Unless we, therefore, recognize the runners in the race as believers, we shall miss the entire lesson. We run because we are saved, not to obtain salvation. What a tragedy it would be if it were not so, for then the weak and halt and crippled would not have a chance of gaining heaven. These Hebrew

Christians too would be shut out, for they were still babes, on the milk bottle. They certainly could not run in a race. And that is just the point in this epistle. It is an impassioned plea to grow up into maturity and give a good account of themselves in the race.

THE WITNESSES

Having identified the contestants in the race, we turn now to the witnesses and spectators in the stands. The verse begins with the word "wherefore" which will help to identify these spectators. The "wherefore" connects this chapter with the previous chapter, and refers to the roster of heroes of the faith from Abel on. Among them are such famous all-stars as Enoch, Noah, Abraham, Jacob, Gideon, Samson, Daniel and many others. The great company consists of past contestants in the race, all letter men, who have finished the course, and are now waiting for the last runner to finish the race, and then the prizes will be given. The stands from which they observe the race is heaven. They are referred to as a "cloud" in the sky. There in heaven are the athletes who, having ended the race, are looking on to encourage us, to warn us and remind us of the rules of the game. The cloud of witnesses is the company of the redeemed ones in heaven.

This raises a question which is constantly asked. Do our loved ones in heaven know what is going on here below? Do they see what we are doing, and how much do they see? There are two views on the matter. First, there are those who believe that the saints in heaven do actually look down upon earth, and are interested in what we are doing. That they do know some things which are happening here below is quite evident, for Jesus says:

> . . . joy shall be in heaven over one sinner that repenteth (Luke 15:7).

This joy is experienced by the saints, for Luke 15:10 says
> . . . there is joy in the *presence* of the angels of God over one sinner that repenteth.

Notice it is not the angels who rejoice, but the joy is in the *presence* of the angels. Those can be none other than the saints in glory. How they receive the news every time a sinner comes to Christ we may not know for certain, but it is possible that they look down upon us here below and observe what we are doing and how we are running the race. What a solemn thought, that our loved ones observe us here below. I often wonder if mother and father are watching me as I struggle and falter along the way. The thought solemnizes me greatly and prompts me to run the race more eagerly, and to refrain from things which I would not want them to see. But how much more solemn the fact about which there is no doubt at all, that God sees all, knows our thoughts and hears every word we speak. God's eye is never closed.

Another interpretation of this cloud of witnesses is almost as solemn. While these saints may not see or know what we are doing here below, their record is a witness from the past that it is possible to win the race and obtain the crown. They overcame and gained the victory, so there can be no excuse for us who have far more light and greater advantages, to fail or fall by the way to "suffer loss," and be "saved so as by fire." Which one of these two interpretations is correct is a matter of personal opinion. Personally, I believe that the saints in heaven do observe what we are doing. How much, we cannot know, but the fact that they do see is a tremendous incentive to press forward in the race, and a powerful deterrent in preventing us from being careless or breaking the rules of the game. But, as stated before, the fact that God sees and knows all should be all-sufficient. This then we believe to be the lesson of:

> Wherefore seeing we also are compassed about with so great a cloud of witnesses . . . (Heb. 12:1).

THE GREAT INCENTIVE

This very fact is given as the great incentive in the race. Because we are compassed about by this great cloud of witnesses, we are admonished:

> . . . let us lay aside every weight and the sin which doth so
> easily beset us, and let us run with patience the race that is set
> before us (Heb. 12:1).

Because of the example of these witnesses and their encouragement, we are to divest ourselves of every encumbrance
which would impede our racing movements in any way. Two
things are mentioned: weights and sins. The runner is to be
properly garbed for the race. It is usually taught that the
weights are a reference to the shedding of all unnecessary
clothing and the putting on of the lightest racing trunks and
shoes. However, there is another thing suggested by weights,
and some interpreters have pointed out that the Greek word
used (*oykon*) means obesity or excess fat, and so teach that the
allusion is to the training required of athletes for getting into
condition by avoiding overweight. They were to observe a
strict diet and by special exercises and rigid discipline reduce
their weight, and develop those muscles needed in the race.
Excess fat was to be reduced to a minimum. The application
is clear as it refers to the Christian. Any encumbrance would
include many things in themselves harmless and innocent, but
if they hinder us in the race, they should be laid aside. Fat
speaks of the excess pleasure and unnecessary luxuries of life.

In the case of the Hebrew Christians it would include old
associations of their former life, lingering Jewish and legal
attachments, the tendency to compromise with the fulfilled
rituals and ceremonialism of the law, and failure to separate from
unbelievers. For us, in addition to these the weights which
hinder us may be the otherwise harmless associations and activities of life, indulged to an excess thus resulting in slowing
us down. The indulgence in innocent pleasures of life may
become a hindrance; in fact, any legitimate enjoyment can become a weight. There is no harm in fishing, but if every spare
moment is given to this sport, to the neglect of one's family,
and if it interferes with one's study of the Word and prayer
and witnessing, it becomes a weight and a sin.

If one works only to make money and lives for the luxuries of life, the best car, the nicest home, and time for enjoyment of the body, it becomes an inexcusable weight. There is nothing wrong with making money, if we realize God has given us the ability to make money, and it belongs to Him, and should be returned to Him, and used for His work and service. For one who has a sedentary occupation and plays golf for exercise, we would not classify his playing the game as a sin, but when the Christian becomes such a golfbug that he has little or no time for spiritual exercises to develop his soul, it becomes a sinful weight. I know Christians who can name every baseball player on all the major league teams, but would be unable to name the books of the New Testament even if their life depended on it.

Your business can become a weight. If you are so busy that you have no time for prayer, Bible study and spiritual service, you are too busy. If your business interferes with your spiritual growth and development, get rid of your business, and trust God instead of your brains. If the average believer would spend half as much time in the Word, in worship, in prayer, as he does in his social activities he would set the world on fire. If the average believer spent as much time with the Bible as he does watching television, you couldn't hold him down. If we would pay as much attention to our spiritual diet as to our physical diet, we would not be such weak, powerless, undernourished, dyspeptic, anemic, enervated spiritual invalids. This is the age of diets, calories, vitamins and health foods. Everyone is concerned about health and vitality, and the best of foods are demanded. Yet too many Christians feed on the husks of the world and neglect the meat of the Word, without a serious thought as to the results.

Let me ask you, how much time did you spend this past week reading the magazines, trade journals, newspapers, novels, market reports and other secular literature? And how much time did you spend feeding your soul on the Word?

Oh, Christians, awake! You are in a race which calls for the best that is in you. What is the weight which is slowing you down in your Christian life? I may not have put my finger on your particular deposit of excess fat, but you know what it is. Ask yourself in everything you do, Does this help or hinder my spiritual life? It really isn't hard if we are only willing to face it. What a disappointment it will be when we meet the Judge of the race and miss the crown and our Lord's commendation. Athletes today as well as in ancient times would deny themselves everything, submit to the severest discipline in training, observe the strictest abstinence and separation from everything which might prevent them from being at the very peak of condition. And they, says Paul,

> . . . do it to obtain a corruptible crown; but we an incorruptible.
>
> I therefore so run, not as uncertainly; so fight I, not as one that beateth the air:
>
> But I keep under my body, and bring it into subjection: lest that by any means, when I have preached to others, I myself should be a castaway [disapproved for a crown] (I Cor. 9:25-27).
>
> So run, that ye may obtain (I Cor. 9:24).

CHAPTER TWENTY-ONE

Disciplined for Service

> For whom the Lord loveth he chasteneth, and scourgeth every son whom he receiveth (Heb. 12:6).

THE Christian life is compared to a race in which all believers are contestants, but all do not win the coveted prize. The race track is here on earth, and the spectators are the saints in heaven who have already finished their course. They are interested onlookers, veterans who are seated in the grandstands of heaven. At the goal line sits the Judge who will present the prizes when all the contestants have crossed the finish line. This is the picture presented to us in Hebrews 12:1, 2:

> Wherefore seeing we also are compassed about with so great a cloud of witnesses, let us lay aside every weight, and the sin which doth so easily beset us, and let us run with patience the race that is set before us,
>
> Looking unto Jesus the author and finisher of our faith; who for the joy that was set before him endured the cross, despising the shame, and is set down at the right hand of the throne of God.

But why are these spectators in heaven so interested in our race here below? The answer is given in the closing verses of chapter eleven. These retired runners will not receive their crowns and rewards until we have all crossed the goal and finished the course. Only after all have concluded the race and all the records are complete will the awarding take place. Of these spectators it is therefore said:

> And these all, having obtained a good report through faith, received not the promise [reward]:

> God having provided some better thing for us, that they with-
> out us should not be made perfect [complete] (Heb. 11:39, 40).

When the last runner in this Church Age has crossed the
line, then our Coach and Leader and Judge will shout from
the air, assemble all the contestants in resurrection bodies to
the Judgment Seat, where each one will be rewarded on the
basis of all the records, taking into consideration the handicaps
and hurdles of the way. Then shall each be rewarded according to his faithfulness. And everyone will be perfectly
satisfied with the decision of the Judge, for it will be in perfect justice and righteousness. Let us wait, therefore, before
we find fault with the way others are running the race, for
we do not know the handicaps under which our brother is
running the race.

> Therefore judge nothing before the time, until the Lord come,
> who both will bring to light the hidden things of darkness [ob-
> stacles we know nothing about], and will make manifest the
> counsels of the hearts [the sincerity with which we ran — not
> our apparent success]: and then shall every man have praise
> of God (I Cor. 4:5).

The important question is, How am I running the race?
The instructions are clear, and there can be no excuse if we
fail to finish the course with joy. The first rule we saw was
separation. We are to "lay aside every weight"; reduce by
getting rid of any hindrance which may impede us. And then
are mentioned the sins which do "so easily beset us." These
are things which are evil in themselves, in contrast to weights
which are not so, but may become sins if allowed to interfere
with our winning the prize.

A third important rule is given next:

> Looking unto Jesus the author and finisher of our faith; who
> for the joy that was set before him endured the cross, despising
> the shame, and is set down at the right hand of the throne of
> God (Heb. 12:2).

We are to keep our eye on the Coach and our ears open to
His directions. We are not to listen to the cheering crowd or

look to see how others are running. Only as we keep before us the example of Jesus can we obtain. He has set the pace, He has successfully run the race before us, and knows every temptation and obstacle in our path. He spared nothing to procure our salvation and the privilege of entering the race. He held back nothing, but He endured the Cross, the ugliest symbol of rejection and reproach. The Cross was the symbol of shame and death. But He despised it all that we might be saved. If we get our eyes off Him and become occupied with self-pity and weariness, we will fail to attain the highest prize. We are therefore urged to

> Consider him that endured such contradiction of sinners against himself, lest ye be wearied and faint in your minds.
> Ye have not yet resisted unto blood, striving against sin (Heb. 12:3, 4).

Compare your sufferings for His sake with His suffering for you, and you will be ashamed of yourself for ever complaining or repining. It has not yet cost us our blood. We have not yet suffered anything by comparison for our stand for Christ. Lost a few friends? Yes. Made fun of and despised? Yes. Suffered material loss for our testimony? Probably. But have they ever stripped you and beaten you? Have they ever put a crown of thorns on your head? Has anyone ever spit in your face because of your faithfulness to Christ? Have your hands and feet ever been nailed to a cross? How insignificant the puny sacrifices we are called to make! Laying aside some easily dispensable weights of a social, material or religious nature, and giving up sins which scar and curse the soul are not sacrifices. What if you would have to pay the price of the martyrs, the faithful missionaries, the saints of former days who sealed their testimony with their blood! It seems to me that it should be easy to say in the light of this:

> All to Jesus I surrender;
> All to leave and follow Thee

Now Comes Chastening

But refusal to obey by voluntarily laying aside every weight and sin does not stop our Captain in His purpose to make us like Himself. He now comes to teach and further train us by chastening.

> For whom the Lord loveth he chasteneth, and scourgeth every son whom he receiveth.
>
> If ye endure chastening, God dealeth with you as with sons; for what son is he whom the father chasteneth not?
>
> But if ye be without chastisement, whereof all are partakers, then are ye bastards, and not sons.
>
> Furthermore we have had fathers of our flesh which corrected us, and we gave them reverence: shall we not much rather be in subjection unto the Father of spirits, and live?
>
> For they verily for a few days chastened us after their own pleasure; but we for our profit, that we might be partakers of his holiness (Heb. 12:6-10).

Whom He Loveth

The Lord chasteneth whom He loveth. How many people imagine when they are chastened that God is angry with them for some wrong, sin or mistake. The chastening may indeed be because of some sin, but it still is His great love which seeks to correct us. God says He chasteneth every son whom he receiveth. Chastening is part of our indispensable training to win the race. Thank God for chastening and what it does. How much better to be chastened no matter how severely, than to be disowned by Him and be lost again. All chastening is for our own good. A number of reasons for chastening are given in our Scripture. Notice the following. Chastening is:

1. Evidence that we are saved (vv. 6-8).
2. For our profit and welfare (v. 10).
3. For our cleansing from sin (v. 11).
4. To prevent us losing our crown (v. 15).

Chastening is first of all evidence that we belong to God's family.

> If ye endure chastening, God dealeth with you as with sons (Heb. 12:7).

God does not chasten the devil's children. He lets them go, and will deal with them in the final judgment, to be cast into the Lake of Fire.

The second purpose of chastening is for our profit. It is God's way of teaching us the unimportance of the temporal and material, and the value of the spiritual, that we might be partakers of His holiness. This is practical holiness. Our positional holiness was settled by the new birth when we believed, but practical holiness, a life of separation and dedication to Him, comes by discipline and chastening.

Thirdly, chastening is for our cleansing and for the producing of righteousness in our lives. The word "chastening" means to make chaste, which means to be pure. God demands that His people shall be clean, and will never stop until this purpose is accomplished. This cleansing can be accomplished in three ways: the gentle way, the severe way and the extreme way. The gentle way is by confession of our sins (I John 1:9). If this is refused, then God may come with present severe chastening of weakness and sickness (I Cor. 11:30); and if this fails, the most extreme means may be used — an untimely death, removal of His child, resulting in his suffering loss at the Judgment Seat of Christ. These three ways are suggested by the three words used in Hebrews 12:5, 6: *rebuke, chastening,* and *scourging.*

God rebukes us through His Word, and

> If we confess our sins, he is faithful and just to forgive us our sins, and to cleanse us from all unrighteousness (I John 1:9).

But rebuke failing, God may take the next step in chastening, so clearly set forth in I Corinthians eleven.

> But let a man examine himself, and so let him eat of that bread, and drink of that cup.
>
> For he that eateth and drinketh unworthily [by refusal to examine self and confess all sin], eateth and drinketh damnation

[judgment, *krineis* in the Greek] to himself, not discerning the Lord's body.

For this cause many are weak and sickly among you, and many sleep.

For if we would judge ourselves, we should not be judged.

But when we are judged, we are *chastened of the Lord*, that we should *not* be condemned with the world (I Cor. 11:28-32).

The meaning is clear. Refusal to confess and repent of all known sin after self-examination makes it necessary for the Lord to step in by chastening. He sends weakness and sickness to correct the erring saint. But if this fails, God may take the extreme method, remove that believer by death, and deal with him at the Judgment Seat of Christ, where:

If any man's work shall be burned, he shall suffer loss: but he himself shall be saved; yet so as by fire (I Cor. 3:15).

Notice how this is also the teaching of Hebrews twelve:

Now no chastening for the present seemeth to be joyous, but grievous: nevertheless afterward it yieldeth the peaceable fruit of righteousness unto them which are exercised thereby (Heb. 12:11).

Notice that last phrase. Chastening yieldeth the peaceable fruit of righteousness. But this is not true of all who are chastened; only those who are exercised thereby, those who learn their lesson and do something about it. But what about those who are *not* exercised by God's chastening, who instead of repenting become bitter and rebellious and find fault with God's dealing with them? What about such? He will have to deal with them later on, at the Judgment Seat.

But there is no need of this extreme dealing, for God has made the way perfectly clear. We have a great High Priest who is waiting even now to forgive, cleanse, restore, refill for service and promise a crown for faithfulness. Before we leave this aspect of our subject we must remind you that not all chastening is because of unconfessed sin. There are many other reasons why God's children suffer, such as to teach us patience, to make us trust Him more, to make us more sympathetic to others, to give us time for prayer, to be an example of patient suffering as a testimony to God's sustaining grace. There are other reasons why God's people pass through many deep experiences. But the one underlying reason is because He loves us, and sends tribulation for "our profit." If you have honestly searched your heart for any known or doubtful sin and confessed it to Him, and yet you are subject to God's chastening, then rejoice that God sees the gold in you which justifies the refining. Let us remember Peter's words:

Beloved, think it not strange concerning the fiery trial which is to try you, as though some strange thing happened unto you:

But rejoice, inasmuch as ye are partakers of Christ's sufferings: that, when his glory shall be revealed, ye may be glad also with exceeding joy.

If ye be reproached for the name of Christ, happy are ye; for the spirit of glory and of God resteth upon you: on their part he is evil spoken of, but on your part he is glorified.

But let none of you suffer as a murderer, or as a thief, or as an evildoer, or as a busybody in other men's matters.

Yet if any man suffer as a Christian, let him not be ashamed; but let him glorify God on this behalf.

For the time is come that judgment must begin at the house of God: and if it first begin at us, what shall the end be of them that obey not the gospel of God (I Pet. 4:12-17).

CHAPTER TWENTY-TWO

Afterward

Now no chastening for the present seemeth to be joyous, but grievous: nevertheless afterward it yieldeth the peaceable fruit of righteousness unto them which are exercised thereby (Heb. 12:11).

THE important key word in this verse is *afterward.* It points to the future, after we have finished the race, and looking back, find the answer to all God's mysterious dealings in sending upon us the trials, testings, tribulations and chastenings which today seem so unexplainable and meaningless. Then we shall fully comprehend the wisdom of God in dealing with us so severely, and rejoice in the great fact of Romans 8:28, "that all things work together for good." All our questions will be answered and the reason for all our trials be made plain.

Why do Christians suffer? Why must we suffer disappointment, loss and pain? Why does God seldom leave us to just quietly enjoy life, without being stirred up by Him again and again? These are questions constantly being asked. There are many, many reasons, but all of them can be gathered up in the one word, *afterward.* All our present experiences have a definite bearing upon the afterward of God. He sees the end from the beginning. When God saved us it was with a definite future goal. It was more than saving us from hell and taking us to heaven when we die. His purpose in saving us was that we might bring forth fruit for the *afterward.* Jesus said:

> Ye have not chosen me, but I have chosen you, and ordained
> you, that ye should go and bring forth fruit, and that your fruit
> should remain (John 15:16).

God does not want us to be barren but fruitful. This means plowing, dragging, pruning and pulling out of weeds. But bringing forth fruit also means growth, progressive development from a tender seedling to the mature plant, for the plant does not produce fruit until it is mature. This is the burden of the whole Epistle to the Hebrews, a plea for these spiritual infants to go on to maturity. The charge against them was that they had remained spiritual babes, subsisting on milk, and needed to be cultivated and brought to fruitfulness.

God's Purpose for Us

God will not cease to deal with us until this maturity is attained. Paul tells us the final result of His dealing with us:

> For whom he did foreknow, them he also did predestinate to
> be conformed to the image of his Son (Rom. 8:29).

God wants us to be like Jesus in the end. He must bring us to perfection. If necessary He uses the severest methods of chastening, but it is all for our profit, that we should be partakers of His holiness. Perfection is the goal, "and holiness, without which no man shall see the Lord." Before we are fit to reign with Him every stain and blot must be removed even though it has to be burned out by the most grievous chastening, or ultimately in the fires of the Judgment Seat of Christ.

In Paul's letter to the Ephesians he says:

> Husbands, love your wives, even as Christ also loved the
> church, and gave himself for it;
> That he might sanctify and cleanse it with the washing of the
> water by the word,
> That he might present it to himself a glorious church, not
> having spot, or wrinkle, or any such thing; but that it should be
> holy and without blemish (Eph. 5:25-27).

Notice again God's *afterward*. It is that He might present it in the afterward without spot or wrinkle. And how does He do it? By sanctifying and cleansing. Two words are used, "sanctify" and "cleanse." The word "sanctify" means making clean by repentance and confession and claiming the word of promise in I John 1:9. But "cleanse" is another word which in the original Greek is *catharesis* from which our English word "cathartic" comes. If we refuse God's gentle washing by the water of the Word, then He must apply sterner measures, and administers a purge, a cathartic, for God wants His people clean.

Again this looks to the *afterward*, for the purpose is stated:

> That he might present it . . . without spot, or wrinkle.

Again two words — "spots" and "wrinkles." Spots are accidental, the result of carelessness, but can be removed by washing in water. For these the water of the Word is provided. But wrinkles are another thing. Wrinkles are the result of inactivity. They result from sitting in one position too long. My clothes do not wrinkle when I stand erect or walk about. But when I lie down in my clothes, or sit with my arms folded and knees crossed, then wrinkles result. And these can be removed, not by mere washing in water, but they need a hot iron.

If we become defiled in our service for Him, and in our eagerness to be busy we become spotted, God understands, and is ready to cleanse when we confess. He is patient with those who stumble and blunder about in their efforts to serve the Lord, just so long as they do something. But inactivity, doing nothing, is inexcusable and will be severely dealt with by the Lord. It is better to make mistakes and bungle things than not to do anything at all. As long as we stumble forward it is better than making no progress at all. And so to remove the wrinkles of our spiritual laziness God applies the hot iron of chastening to stir us into activity. The infants, the perpetual babies of Hebrews must *go on to* perfection.

LIFT UP THE HANDS

> Wherefore lift up the hands which hang down, and the feeble knees (Heb. 12:12).

Get going! Don't just sit there. Do something. Start running the race.

> And make straight paths for your feet, lest that which is lame be turned out of the way; but let it rather be healed.
>
> Follow peace with all men, and holiness, without which no man shall see the Lord:
>
> Looking diligently lest any man fail of the grace of God; lest any root of bitterness springing up trouble you, and thereby many be defiled (Heb. 12:13-15).

The chastening of the Lord is designed to produce cleansing, sweetness, holiness and peace. But where the chastening is despised, bitterness is the result. If being often warned, and constantly chastened of the Lord, the believer persists in his unrepentance, and becomes bitter instead of sweet, he may be left alone at the place where it is "impossible" to renew him to repentance, to await his terrible loss at the Judgment Seat of Christ.

THE CASE OF ESAU

The case of Esau's futile search for repentance is inserted as an illustration. It is a solemn warning against sinning deliberately and against better light.

> Lest there be any fornicator or profane person, as Esau, who for one morsel of meat sold his birthright.
>
> For ye know how that afterward, when he would have inherited the blessing, he was rejected: for he found no place of repentance, though he sought it carefully with tears (Heb. 12:16, 17).

These verses do not teach that Esau was saved and then again was lost. It is only an illustration of the danger of missing the blessing for the love of the material and the physical pleasures of this life. Esau did not look to the *afterward*, but lived only for the present, and when later he realized his error, he sought the blessing, but was refused because he *did not repent*. The translation makes it seem as though Esau sought repentance with tears, but the original indicates he sought the lost blessing which he had sold for a morsel of food. It should read,

> Afterward when he again wanted the blessing, he was refused, though he sought it [the blessing] carefully with tears, for he had no place for repentance.

THE PERSPECTIVE

The secret of the victorious life, and running the race successfully is a matter of perspective. It is keeping before us the *afterward*, looking unto Jesus, keeping our eye on the prize. Chapter twelve of Hebrews closes with this perspective. These Hebrew Christians were tempted to go back to the beggarly elements of the law, and place themselves under bondage to escape a little present discomfort, reproach and persecution. In order to urge them on, a contrast between the law and grace, Mount Sinai and Calvary, is now presented:

> For ye are not come unto the mount that might be touched, and that burned with fire, nor unto blackness, and darkness, and tempest,
> And the sound of a trumpet, and the voice of words; which voice they that heard intreated that the word should not be spoken to them any more:
> (For they could not endure that which was commanded, And if so much as a beast touch the mountain, it shall be stoned, or thrust through with a dart:
> And so terrible was the sight, that Moses said, I exceedingly fear and quake) (Heb. 12:18-21).

Here is a picture of the law and its condemnation. The law said, *stay away, do not trespass*. Death awaits you under the law. The law condemns the sinner, it engenders fear and trembling. The law exposed sin but could not take it away. The law revealed judgment but could not save. The law demanded perfection, but could not produce perfection. The law demanded obedience but could not help the sinner to be obedient. The law was never meant to save anyone. God never expected any mere human being to keep that law. When He gave the law and demanded obedience He knew that no one would keep it, nay more, He knew no sinner *could* keep it. God demanded of Israel something they were totally powerless to do. Shall we then accuse God of unrighteousness? Is He a God of caprice? Ah, no! The law was not intended to save, but instead was given to prove the utter helplessness of man to be saved by his works of the law, in order that he might abandon all hope of saving himself, and turn to Jesus only for salvation. What the law could not do, Jesus did.

> For what the law could not do, in that it was weak through the flesh, God sending his own Son in the likeness of sinful flesh, and for sin, condemned sin in the flesh:
> That the righteousness of the law might be fulfilled in us [not by us], who walk not after the flesh, but after the Spirit (Rom. 8:3, 4).

Imagine these Hebrew Christians wanting to place themselves again under the law. Now notice the folly of such error when we contrast Israel under the law with the believer under grace.

> And to Jesus the mediator of the new covenant, and to the blood of sprinkling, that speaketh better things than that of Abel (Heb. 12:24).

This is the heritage of believers. What then shall we say of those who would go back to the law, after they are saved? To imagine that we can be saved by grace, and then be kept by our works, is to go back from liberty to bondage. It is the evidence of spiritual infancy. Spiritual maturity comes only when we abandon all hope not only of saving ourselves, but also of keeping ourselves. When we sin, God has made provision for cleansing. The chapter ends with a solemn warning.

> For our God is a consuming fire (Heb. 12:29).

Afterward! We look forward to this unshakable kingdom.

> Wherefore we receiving a kingdom which cannot be moved, let us have grace [not law], whereby we may serve God acceptably with reverence and godly fear:
> For our God is a consuming fire (Heb. 12:28,29).

CHAPTER TWENTY-THREE

Your Report Card

Let brotherly love continue (Heb. 13:1).

AT the close of a school semester, or upon completion of a prescribed course of study it is customary for the teachers to subject the students to a test or examination to determine how much the pupil has absorbed and retained of that which was taught in the daily class sessions. The results of these finals have an important bearing on the final grade, and may determine whether the individual will pass or not. No matter how brilliant the student may have been in his daily assignments, if he "flunks" his final, it will pull his average down, for the term's marks are determined largely on the final examination. Some students are like a sieve, knowledge just runs through; others are reservoirs for the storing up of knowledge as a source of refreshing and power for the future.

We can apply this method to the study of the Bible. As you read the epistles, you will notice that as a rule several chapters are devoted to the doctrinal teaching of the Word, and then the last chapter or chapters are devoted to a practical application of these truths, to be translated into action. Such is the case in the Book of Hebrews. The first twelve chapters compose the doctrinal section, dealing with many of the deepest, most fundamental and weighty truths of the Word. The charge against these Hebrew Christians was that they had made so little progress that they were still in the kindergarten, whereas they should be completing their "teacher train-

183

ing course." We repeat the complaint against them in Hebrews 5:12,

> For when . . . ye ought to be teachers, ye have need that one teach you again which be the first principles of the oracles of God; and are become such as have need of milk, and not of strong meat.

And, therefore, the advice follows:

> Therefore leaving the principles of the doctrine of Christ, let us go on to perfection [maturity] (Heb. 6:1).

This solid meat is then dished out to them, and the epistle sets forth the great doctrines of the superiority of Christ, His Deity, His priestly ministry, the victorious life, the believer's security, the doctrine of rewards, the sin unto death, the Judgment Seat of Christ, the power of faith and the ministry of chastening. Now the course is completed and the examination follows in the closing chapter. Hebrews thirteen is the final examination at the end of the course.

The test is in the form of a quiz program, where the student is presented with a set of suggested questions and permitted to grade himself. The examination opens with a statement.

> Let brotherly love continue (Heb. 13:1).

We should like to put it in the form of a question, "Has your brotherly love continued?" It is assumed that you began with some brotherly love, but have these studies increased or diminished your love? Continuation implies progress, advancement, growth and increase. And this is the leading question of this examination chapter. All the other answers to the other questions will be largely determined by your answer to this one. What is your answer? How has your love for the brethren been affected by these studies?

As you have listened to and studied these expositions on Hebrews, what has it done for you? From the mail we have received it is evident that instead of causing some of you to love me more, it has been the exact opposite. The attitude of some was condemnatory, and some of it even abusive, because my interpretation of Hebrews went counter to your traditional understanding and interpretation of the Book of Hebrews. You could not agree with me at all, and told me so in no uncertain terms. I appreciate your frankness, I welcome criticism, I am always open to valid arguments and eager to change my views if they are proven in error. But this criticism must always be carried on in love. No matter how much we as brethren may disagree, we must do so without becoming disagreeable. If your disagreement makes you disagreeable instead of continuing in brotherly love, I am frank to say I take your disagreement lightly.

Not Force Our Ideas

The important thing is not that we should agree on everything in the Bible, but if our differences of opinion drive us to the Book, prompt us to pray for each other, and provoke us to deeper searching of the truth to see if these things be so, then there will be a blessing for both of us. Then whether we agree or not is of minor importance. But by all means "Let brotherly love continue." This does not mean we cannot love a brother unless he agrees in everything with us. I thank God for disagreements and differences of opinion. What a drab life it would be if it were not so. I cannot imagine how there could be any joy in living with anyone who did not have a mind of his own. Take my wife, for instance. I love her, not only in spite of the fact she has ideas contrary to mine, but I love her all the more because she isn't a wishy-washy "jellyfish" who never dares to disagree with me. She doesn't know how proud I am inside, when in opposing some of my wild ideas, her eyes flash and she tries to set me straight. I know she does it because she loves me, and vice versa. How unbearably monotonous it would be if she always agreed with me, "Yes, papa; yes, daddy; yes, dearie." Married life would lose much of its zest and spice if there would not be two minds, but how blessed when these two different minds can work together in love. Someone has said, "Husband and wife are one in heart, but not always of one mind."

Brother, how did you do on the first question of your test? Can you still love me though you think I am all wrong? Think how wrong you were, when Christ loved you enough to die for you.

> God commendeth his love toward us, in that while we were yet sinners Christ died for us.

HOSPITALITY

The second test of our Christian growth is given in verse two:

> Be not forgetful to entertain strangers: for thereby some have entertained angels unawares (Heb. 13:2).

This does not mean careless and foolish entertainment of any stranger who seeks to enter our homes. It applies definitely to "brethren" whom we have not personally met before. The word "stranger" is *philonexia* meaning "dear ones." It looks back to verse one, "Let brotherly love continue." It speaks of hospitality to the brethren, even though they may be strangers.

The third test of brotherly love is sympathy.

> Remember them that are in bonds, as bound with them; and them which suffer adversity as being yourselves also in the body (Heb. 13:3).

Today in this age of "dog eat dog" and "everyone for himself," this admonition is sorely needed. How little we appreciate the loneliness and grief of those who are ill and bereaved. We have time for recreation, sports and pleasures, for social entertainment and business, but how little time to visit and comfort the less fortunate among God's people. Pure religion and undefiled, says James, is to "visit the widows and fatherless," and to keep ourselves unspotted from the world. Think of the joy and happiness you could bring to some lonely heart today by just a visit to break up the long, weary hours. Remember those who are in trouble, sorrow and perplexity.

IN THE HOME

Next follows a real test. How does your faith affect your home life? Nowhere can we form a better estimate of a man's faith than in the home. And so Hebrews 13:4 says:

> Marriage is honourable in all, and the bed undefiled: but whore-mongers and adulterers God will judge.

The free rendering of this verse may be given as follows: "Let your marriage be honorable, and keep it pure and undefiled."

Purity in the home, the husband honoring the wife, and the wife reverencing her husband, should be the norm for every Christian home. Husbands and wives can live in love and harmony, and solve all their difficulties if they will but heed one single verse of Scripture:

> And be ye kind one to another, tenderhearted, forgiving one another even as God for Christ's sake hath forgiven you (Eph. 4:32).

Some time ago a woman called me on the phone pleading with me to come over immediately, for their home was threatened with disaster. She and her husband had been quarreling and feuding for months, and now it had come to a crisis and he was preparing to leave after she had threatened to divorce him. "Oh, do come over and save our home," she cried. After she quieted sufficiently for me to get in a word, I said, "Are you a Christian?"

She replied, "Yes."

"And is your husband a Christian?"

She again said, "Yes, he is, and he is listening on the other phone and wants to tell you his side of the story. Please do come over."

"I am willing to come over," I said, "but only after you do just one thing. You are both Christians, you say. Then you believe God's Word. In that Word you have the solution to your problem, and if you will not let God solve it, I am sure

I cannot do anything for you. Sit down and take your Bible, and read together this verse, Ephesians 4:32,

> And be ye kind one to another, tenderhearted, forgiving one another, even as God for Christ's sake hath forgiven you.

There is God's remedy for your problem. Just obey that verse and you won't need me or anyone else to fix up your troubles. Try this first, and if it doesn't work, call me." They never called again, but weeks later when we met, they told how the simple formula of Ephesians 4:32 brought peace and love.

CONTENTMENT

The next fruit of our growth in grace is contentment.

> Let your conversation be without covetousness; and be content with such things as ye have: for he hath said, I will never leave thee, nor forsake thee,
> So that we may boldly say, The Lord is my helper, and I will not fear what man shall do unto me (Heb. 13:5, 6).

The most miserable people I have ever met were those who had great wealth and could buy anything their hearts desired, but who in spite of this were as unhappy as they could be. The happiest folks I have ever met were sufferers upon sickbeds; those sweet Christians afflicted and tried, and yet rejoicing in the Lord.

Finally we have the admonition to pray for those whom God has appointed to rule in the assembly and to preach the Word.

> Remember them which have the rule over you, who have spoken unto you the word of God: whose faith follow, considering the end of their conversation.
> Jesus Christ the same yesterday, and to day, and for ever (Heb. 13:7, 8).

This section closes with an admonition not to be carried away with divers and strange doctrines. This indeed is up-to-date advice. We are living in the days of which Jesus said, "Take heed that no man deceive you by any means." There is no period in the history of God's people when there has been as much deception and false doctrine abroad as today. The past few years have seen the multiplication of sects and cults and religions of every conceivable sort. They arise overnight, and come with some of the most fantastic, fanatical, unearthly doctrines and teachings, manifestations and delusions. Never before has there been such confusion of tongues, so many strange voices saying, "Here is the truth." They quote Scripture, claim supernatural powers, prattle about faith, promise healing, health and wealth, while leaving behind a veritable stream of disillusioned, disappointed, frustrated souls. And no matter how wild the fire, if it is only accompanied by a little Scripture, these cults do not lack for followers. While they piously quote the Scripture, "Jesus Christ the same yesterday, and to day, and for ever," they misinterpret its message in practice. We ask, Why are Christians so gullible? Why are they so easily fooled? We come right back to the case of the people in the Book of Hebrews. They were weaklings, babes, undernourished infants. The only antidote against the deceptions of this day is *the Word*, the *solid meat of the Word*. Unless we saturate ourselves in the Word, and become mature through the strong meat of Scripture, we shall not be able to stand. How solemn, therefore the words in II Peter:

But there were false prophets also among the people, even as there shall be false teachers among you, who privily shall bring in damnable heresies, even denying the Lord that bought them, and bring upon themselves swift destruction.

And many shall follow their pernicious ways; by reason of whom the way of truth shall be evil spoken of.

And through covetousness shall they with feigned words make merchandise of you: whose judgment now of a long time lingereth not, and their damnation slumbereth not. (II Pet. 2:1-3).

Don't be fooled by pious promises and smooth words, but heed our Saviour's words in Matthew seven:

Beware of false prophets, which come to you in sheep's clothing, but inwardly they are ravening wolves (Matt. 7:15).

> Not every one that saith unto me, Lord, Lord, shall enter into the kingdom of heaven; but he that doeth the will of my Father which is in heaven.
>
> Many will say to me in that day, Lord, Lord, have we not prophesied in thy name? and in thy name have cast out devils? and in thy name done many wonderful works?
>
> And then will I profess unto them, I never knew you: depart from me, ye that work iniquity (Matt. 7:21-32).

Check everything by the Word. Let no man deceive you by any means. It is the sign of the end time and so great will the deception become that if it were possible, the very elect of God would be deceived (Matt. 24:24).

> For false Christs and false prophets shall rise, and shall shew signs and wonders, to seduce, if it were possible, even the elect.
>
> But take ye heed: behold, I have foretold you all things (Mark 13:22, 23).

CHAPTER TWENTY-FOUR
Be Ye Separate

> We have an altar, whereof they have no right to eat which serve the tabernacle.
>
> For the bodies of those beasts, whose blood is brought into the sanctuary by the high priest for sin, are burned without the camp.
>
> Wherefore Jesus also, that he might sanctify the people with his own blood, suffered without the gate.
>
> Let us go forth therefore unto him without the camp, bearing his reproach.
>
> For here we have no continuing city, but we seek one to come (Heb. 13:10-14).

HEBREWS thirteen is the practical application of the teachings of this wonderful epistle of assurance. Because of the full and adequate provision made for both our justification and sanctification, He expects of us the fruits of the Spirit. These fruits are enumerated in this chapter beginning with brotherly love. The chapter opens with

> Let brotherly love continue (Heb. 13:1).

This brotherly love is manifested by:
1. Hospitality (v. 2).
2. Sympathy (v. 3).
3. Personal purity (v. 4).
4. Contentment (v. 5).
5. Confidence (v. 6).
6. Intercession (v. 7).
7. Stability (v. 9).

Separation

And now comes the next mark of the Christian — separation from the world. Reference is made to the offering of the Tabernacle where the blood of the burnt offering was sprinkled upon the furniture of the Tabernacle, but the bodies of the sacrifice were killed outside the camp itself. Of this the Old Testament priest had no right to partake. But we today are privileged to partake to the full of the Antitype of these offerings, the Lord Jesus Christ, who was slain as God's final offering outside the walls of Jerusalem. It was the place of rejection and separation. Because of the example of our Lord we are now admonished to take our place with Jesus outside the camp in the place of reproach and rejection. This is the force of the words:

> Let us go forth therefore unto him without the camp, bearing his reproach (Heb. 13:13).

Jesus Christ is still without the camp. He is still the rejected one of the world. If we are to follow Him, we too must be willing to go outside the camp and bear His reproach. It is the only place where the real Jesus is to be found. The camp in our Scripture was the city of Jerusalem, the religious center of that day. The services in the Temple had degenerated into an empty, hollow traditional system of dead religion. The priests who slew the sacrifices had rejected God's Lamb. The doctors of the law who were to teach the people had crucified God's Son. The Pharisees who boasted of their orthodoxy had demanded the death of the Saviour. And so they denied Him a place even to die in the city, and instead bore Him outside the city walls to Golgotha.

The camp, therefore, represented a corrupted religious system of forms, rituals and ceremonies, a religion which went through all the motions but rejected the Son of God. Today it represents anything religious which denies the Lord Jesus Christ as the supernaturally conceived, virgin-born, sinless Son of God, anything which denies His Deity, His substitu-

tionary atonement, His bodily resurrection and the power of
His cleansing blood. The true believer is to separate himself
from all who deny these basic fundamental truths of redemption and to have no fellowship with the "unfruitful works of
darkness." It is the message of separation — not religious in-
tegration.

Outside the camp was the place of reproach. It was the place
where refuse was dumped as worthless trash. In Leviticus
4:11, 12 we read:

> And the skin of the bullock [the sin offering], and all his flesh,
> with his head, and with his legs, and his inwards, and his dung,
> Even the whole bullock shall he carry forth without the camp
> unto a clean place, where the ashes are poured out, and burn him
> on the wood with fire: where the ashes are poured out shall he be
> burnt.

The camp itself (Jerusalem and its empty religion) had
become an unclean place, unfit for a holy sacrifice, and the
unclean place outside the camp becomes sanctified by the sacrifice of Christ. It became a place of sacrifice and separation
and reproach.

The Call to Separation

Every believer who wishes to follow Christ in absolute
separation from a bloodless religious system will find himself
outside the camp. He will not be popular, but be reproached
for the sake of Christ. The only other alternative is compromise. Now this separation of ourselves does not mean a
"holier than thou," bigoted separation from other believers
who may not belong to our particular sect, denomination or
communion. The Body of Christ is bigger than all these.
The first verse in our chapter takes care of any bigotry or
sectarian self-righteousness, for the chapter begins with

> Let brotherly love continue (Heb. 13:1).

We are to love all those who love our Lord and to love
the enemies of Christ and seek to win them for Him, but
this does not imply we are to endorse their rejection of Christ

or be partakers of their evil doings. To take a separated stand
may mean loss of friends, business, popularity and social position, but it is the path our Saviour trod, and if we are to follow Him it means going

> . . . without the camp, bearing his reproach (Heb. 13:13).

And why? Because we have here no continuing city, but
seek one to come. We are but strangers and pilgrims here,
and the older I become the more I realize I don't fit in with
this old world program.

The same thing is true of modes of dress invented by the
world and avidly copied by Christians. I am not speaking of
unbelievers, but to believers who profess to believe what God
says. God wants us to adorn these bodies which are the
temples of the Holy Spirit. We should keep these temples
clean, and they should be dressed in a way that befits the
temple of God. There is no excuse for being slovenly and
tacky in our dress. We abhor the extremes of a past genera-
tion with its bustles and rats and dresses trailing in the filth
of the streets, but we denounce with even greater vigor the
sensual extremes of today. The shameful abbreviation of dress
with which both men and women appear in public is utterly
unbecoming to Christians. If the world goes to the extremes
of plucking the eyebrows, painting toenails, fingernails like
eagle claws, we have little to say to them — but for Christians
the extremes of these customs are utterly unbecoming. The
Bible is clear in speaking to Christians:

> Whose adorning let it not be that outward adorning of plaiting
> the hair, and of wearing of gold, or of putting on of apparel;
> But let it be the hidden man of the heart, in that which is not
> corruptible, even the ornament of a meek and quiet spirit, which
> is in the sight of God of great price (I Pet. 3:3, 4).

Compare the time you spend on adorning your body with
the time spent in the Word and prayer and testimony, and
you will find the reason for your spiritual immaturity.

And you men, is your life one of separation, in the way

you expose your body in public? Among your friends does your conversation bespeak your Christian profession?

PERSONAL APPLICATION

This we believe to be the primary interpretation of Hebrews 13:10-13. But it goes much farther in its application to our personal relationship in this world. The Lord expects of the believer a life of separation from all evil and questionable habits, associations and entanglements. Unless the world can see in us a difference in the places we frequent, the activities in which we indulge, the language we use and even in the way we dress to avoid the modern extremes of the world, they are not apt to respect our testimony.

We are living in a day when we hear precious little about the truth of personal separation from the world and things of the flesh. The Bible is clear in its admonition,

> Let every one that nameth the name of Christ depart from iniquity (II Tim. 2:19).

And in I Thessalonians 5:22 we are admonished to "Abstain from all appearance of evil." There are some things which are not evil in themselves but may become so if we permit them to become stumblingblocks to others. We are more than individuals; we are members of a society, and therefore the question never is only, "Is it right or wrong?" but "Is this thing pleasing to God, and does it help or hinder others in coming to Christ?" Does the world see Christ in your daily life? Does it see a difference between you and the world? I grant you that you will probably not be popular with the world, but the Bible plainly tells us that

> . . . the friendship of the world is enmity with God? Whosoever therefore will be a friend of the world is the enemy of God (Jas. 4:4).

And John says,

> Love not the world, neither the things that are in the world. If any man love the world, the love of the Father is not in him (I John 2:15).

How we need again the words of Paul in Romans twelve:

> I beseech you therefore, brethren, by the mercies of God, that ye present your bodies a living sacrifice, holy, acceptable unto God, which is your reasonable service.
>
> And be not conformed to this world: but be ye transformed by the renewing of your mind, that ye may prove what is that good, and acceptable, and perfect, will of God (Rom. 12:1, 2).

CHAPTER TWENTY-FIVE

The Fruit of Our Lips

By him therefore let us offer the sacrifice of praise to God continually, that is, the fruit of our lips giving thanks to his name (Heb. 13:15).

HEBREWS thirteen is a basket of beautiful fruits. They are the fruits which the Lord looks for in the life of the believer as a result of his growing in grace, until maturity is reached. The more mature and the healthier the tree, the greater will be the quantity of fruit. As a tree is known by its fruits, so too the progress of the believer in his growth in grace will be evidenced by the amount and quantity of fruits evidenced in daily life. In the first fourteen verses of Hebrews 13, nine fruits are given. These we have briefly discussed in our previous chapters. And now we come to the tenth fruit.

TESTIMONY OF OUR LIPS

It is called the "fruit of our lips," and is defined as the sacrifice of praise to God, giving thanks to His Name. The fruit of our lips then includes more than just giving a testimony at a prayer meeting or on a street corner. It is called a "sacrifice of praise" to God. It is to be "continual," and not sporadic, not reserved only for certain occasions, such as testimony meetings and other special occasions. We are to continue it when we go to work, when we mingle with men socially and in business. It does not necessarily mean giving an oral testimony, but our life and conduct are to be filled with praise and thanksgiving. We can testify without uttering a word. Refusal to indulge in the questionable practices of the crowd can be a testimony without saying a word. A cheery smile when insulted, kindness and patience under persecution, courtesy when rudely reviled — these are the fruits of the sacrifice of praise to God. Bowing one's head to ask grace before a meal in a worldly, ungodly place is as much a testimony as getting up to preach. It is significant that the word "continually" is inserted right in the middle of this verse.

The Sacrifice of Praise

Notice that our testimony, the fruit of our lips, is called a "sacrifice of praise." It means sacrifice; and faithfulness to Christ may cost us something. It is not always easy to be firm and unyielding in the time of temptation, jeering and reviling. It may cost friends, or even one's job, but no sacrifice is too great when viewed in the light of Calvary.

Peter tells us:

> If ye be reproached for the name of Christ, happy are ye; for the spirit of glory and of God resteth upon you: on their part he is evil spoken of, but on your part he is glorified (I Pet. 4:14).

But be sure you suffer for His Name's sake and not for your own foolishness' sake. Even in our testimony we must be wise as serpents and harmless as doves. We can spoil our testimony for Christ by giving it the wrong way, and testifying in the wrong place and the wrong time. I had a friend years ago, now with the Lord, whom I sometimes envied for his zeal and boldness, for his fearlessness in witnessing for Christ. But while his heart was burning and his motives the very best, he lacked sadly in good judgment, and often spoiled his testimony by his untactful conduct. He had more in his heart than in his head. One day he came to me, sad and depressed, because, as he said, he was suffering persecution for Jesus' sake. He said he had lost his job because of his testimony for Christ. Upon investigation however, I found that he had been fired because of his own poor judgment. He worked in an assembly plant and would stop his work to talk to some fellow workman about Jesus or hand out a tract. The boss warned him not to continue the practice, and when he said, "I must obey God rather than man," he was promptly fired.

A LOST TESTIMONY

And he came to me for sympathy. But I asked, "Did you do this during working hours?"

He replied, "Yes, because if I waited it might be too late." As a result he was dismissed and now all opportunity for contact was gone. If he had witnessed and distributed tracts during coffee break or lunch hour, no one could accuse him. But he had agreed when he was hired to give forty hours of work per week for value received. In his zeal he was "stealing" company time. He could have been a far greater testimony by giving his best work, being on time, excelling in the quality of his work, and living a life above criticism. He was not suffering reproach for Christ but paying for his own foolishness. Your testimony will not amount to much until it is backed up by a life above reproach, hence the advice of Peter:

> But let none of you suffer as a murderer, or as a thief, or as an evildoer, or as a busybody in other men's matters.
> Yet if any man suffer as a Christian, let him not be ashamed; but let him glorify God on this behalf (I Pet. 4:15, 16).

Until your words are backed up by works they will convince no one. And that is probably why the admonition to offer the fruit of our lips is not mentioned until after the other fruits are enumerated: love, hospitality, submission, purity, contentment, boldness, sympathy, stability, and finally separation without the camp. All these come first and then our testimony will be believed.

THEIR CHARITY

And then follows the next fruit, "liberality and charity." That is the way to back up your testimony, and the writer continues:

> But to do good and to communicate forget not: for with such sacrifices God is well pleased (Heb. 13:16).

The margin of my Bible renders the word "communicate" thus: "to share what you have with others." A stingy Christian is a contradiction. Covetousness and the love of money are the root of all evil. Unbelievers often put to shame the believers by being far more practically compassionate and liberal. The story is told of a pious deacon who heard of a poor widow in dire material poverty and without food. Remembering that James said pure religion was to visit the fatherless and the widows in their affliction, he visited the poor woman, and getting on his knees began fervently to pray for the Lord to relieve her distress. The window being open, an infidel passing by heard the prayer (for God was evidently not listening to it), and went to a near-by store and purchased a supply of food. When he returned to the widow's house, the deacon was still praying, so he softly lifted the basket through the window on the floor and left the ridiculous prayer meeting. The deacon was still praying. Is not this what James also refers to in James 2:14-16:

> What doth it profit, my brethren, though a man say he hath faith, and have not works? can faith save him?
> If a brother or sister be naked, and destitute of daily food,
> And one of you say unto them, Depart in peace, be ye warmed and filled; notwithstanding ye give them not those things which are needful to the body; what doth it profit?

The world is sick and tired of a lot of pious cant and preaching and is looking for a practical demonstration of the love of Christ. But most important of all it is pleasing to God, for the verse in its entirety reads:

> But to do good and to communicate [share what you have with others] forget not: for with such sacrifices God is well pleased (Heb. 13:16).

Two more fruits are mentioned in Hebrews 13:17, 18:

> Obey them that have the rule over you, and submit yourselves: for they watch for your souls, as they that must give account, that they may do it with joy, and not with grief: for that is unprofitable for you.
> Pray for us: for we trust we have a good conscience, in all things willing to live honestly.

In verse seventeen we have a much-forgotten virtue — respect for those who have been called to guide the flock of God. While all Christians are called to minister in the things of God, there are specially chosen servants, ordained of God, who have been called to rule, oversee, guide and instruct the members of the Body of Christ. They are called elders; ruling elders and teaching elders, also called pastors, teachers and bishops. These demand and deserve the respect and encouragement of the flock in their difficult task. They are not to be exalted for their person's sake but because of the office which they hold. There is today a sad lack of this grace and fruit of the Spirit. When I was a lad we were taught to have respect for the preacher, not because he was a preacher, but because he was an anointed servant of God. In too many circles today this obedience to, and respect for, our elders is almost nonexistent. The minister has become the errand boy and handyman in the congregation. He is called by his first name and his counsel is ignored. We do not mean to infer that a minister is to be exalted above any other member of the Body of Christ because he is better or more worthy in himself, but because God in grace has given him a ministry and an office which demands respect, honor and obedience. All this of course refers only to faithful ministers of the Lord who watch over the souls of the flock "as they that must give account, that they may do it with joy, and not with grief: for that is unprofitable for you."

Instead of criticizing and finding fault with your pastor, spend the time praying for him, helping him by relieving him of some of the numerous details of his work. When you have received blessings, tell him about it. Don't worry that it will puff him up, there are plenty of other things to keep him humble. And finally, support him materially so he can live on the same economic plane as you do, and be relieved of the worry about keeping the wolf from the door. The laborer is worthy of his hire and the husbandman must be partaker of the fruits.

Finally — Prayer

The last but not least of the fruits of mature Christian experience is prayer (Heb. 13:18). It is not left for the last because it is of minor importance, but because it is most important and must not be forgotten. And if these other graces abound, prayers will be more effective.

The epistle closes with a benediction and an apology. The benediction is:

> Now the God of peace, that brought again from the dead our Lord Jesus, that great shepherd of the sheep, through the blood of the everlasting covenant,
> Make you perfect in every good work to do his will, working in you that which is wellpleasing in his sight, through Jesus Christ; to whom be glory for ever and ever. Amen (Heb. 13: 20, 21).

The goal of the Christian life is perfection. In Hebrews five we saw the charge of immaturity brought against these Hebrews. They were children still on a milk diet, devoid of fruit, underdeveloped and stunted. The admonition was "Go on to perfection." Grow up and become mature. Only mature trees bear a maximum of friut. Young trees may blossom profusely but the flowers do not set, and the fruit does not develop. As we come to the close of Hebrews, the fruits of mature Christian development are therefore enumerated beginning with brotherly love and ending with prayer. The benediction which follows is that they may continue to grow and be made perfect in every good work, working that which is wellpleasing in his sight. The expression, "make you perfect," means bring to completion. And the evidence of this Christian maturity is works, and therefore the closing admonition:

> Make you perfect in every good work . . . working in you.

AN APOLOGY

Then follows an apology. It is tender and touching:

> And I beseech you, brethren, suffer the word of exhortation: for I have written a letter unto you in few words (Heb. 13:22).

Suffer the word of exhortation! The exhortation had been pointed and direct. His charge against them of spiritual immaturity, his severe warnings against the sin unto death, his solemn revelation concerning chastening and suffering loss at the Judgment Seat of Christ, were not by any means pleasant or welcome truths, and he fears they may resent the solemn implications of judgment and loss of rewards. They would undoubtedly rather hear about grace, and security and rewards, and their inheritance and position in Christ. They enjoyed hearing about "no condemnation"; but the message on the responsibilities of grace and the announcement that "God shall judge his people," this they would rather not hear. And so the writer apologetically beseeches them to "suffer the word of exhortation."

Things have not changed. The message of grace is popular, but the responsibilities of grace are not so. We hear but little about the Judgment Seat of Christ. We preach on rewards but give little attention to the "loss of rewards," suffering loss and being saved so as by fire. We believe this very tendency has unconsciously been the reason why the solemn warnings in Hebrews have been brushed off and applied to unregenerate religious professors, described as "Jewish professed believers who halt short of faith in Christ, after advancing

to the very threshold of salvation." We are aware that rejecting this venerated traditional position and the application
of the exhortation to ourselves as believers, is not popular.
If you disagree, we shall still love one another. And so I too
would close this volume with the words of Hebrews 13:22.
If these truths have been hard to receive, then

> I beseech you, brethren, suffer the word of exhortation.

Grace be with you all. Amen.

The Judgment Seat of Christ

ANY exposition of Hebrews would be incomplete without an explanatory chapter on the lesser-known and little-understood revelation concerning the Judgment Seat of Christ.

The Judgment Seat of Christ is the answer to the question which Paul anticipated would be raised by his teaching of "salvation by grace" and the "security of the believer." The question is, "Shall we sin that grace may abound?"

Those who teach the doctrine of salvation by grace without the works of the law are constantly accused of promoting license to sin. The doctrine of the security of the believer is severely attacked as a dangerous doctrine, which encourages looseness of living and tends to carelessness, carnality and a false sense of security and peace. The accusations are not without some foundation, and the charges should be faced seriously and met Scripturally. The preaching of salvation wholly by grace, without the counterbalancing teaching of the responsibilities of grace has led many to believe that it makes no difference how we act and live *after* we are saved, because it is "all of grace" and is "all under the blood." There can be no question that too many Christians have given occasion for these accusations. Unless we can give a Scriptural answer, we must admit the criticism is just. What then is our answer to such questions as: Can a Christian once saved go back again into the world? Can he do as he pleases? Does grace give a right to sin? Will God deal with such? How and where will it be done? What will happen to Christians who live and die with unconfessed and unrepented sin?

THE BIBLE ANSWER

We believe the answer is made perfectly clear in the Bible. Hundreds of passages (inexcusably overlooked or ignored by the average student) teach the doctrine of the Judgment Seat of Christ. While the guilt of sin is instantly taken care of, permanently blotted out, when the sinner receives Christ, and he will never be condemned or lost, he nevertheless is responsible for all he does as a believer, and will have to give an account at the Judgment Seat and be rewarded in perfect justice, and be assigned his relative rank and place in the Kingdom, on the basis of the record. This is clear from scores of unmistakable passages, most familiar of which is I Corinthians 3:11-15. In II Corinthians 5:10 Paul says:

> For we must all appear before the judgment seat of Christ; that every one may receive the things done in his body, according to that he hath done, whether it be good or bad.

(See also Matt. 6:6; 10:42; Luke 6:22,35; Col. 3:24; Heb. 11:6; Rev. 22:12.) There will a reckoning for the servants of the Lord (Matt. 25:19).

There are three judgments of the believer mentioned in the Bible: a past, a present and a future judgment. The judgment for the guilt of sin is a settled past fact, assuring the believer's position in Christ, his completed salvation, and his eternal security by the finished work of Christ (John 5:24; 10:28; Rom. 5:1; 8:1). There is also a present judgment of the believer's "walk." To those who continue in unrepented, unconfessed sin, God comes to chasten them by "weakness and sickness and death" (I Cor. 11:29-31). This is not a matter of salvation, but for correction and chastening (I Cor. 11:32; Heb. 12:6). But there is a third judgment which is future.

It has to do with our works, and will determine our rewards for faithfulness, and loss of rewards for unfaithfulness. It has nothing to do with our salvation, but only with rewards.

WHO, WHEN AND WHERE?

Before considering the character of this judgment, we must determine: (1) Who will be present at this judgment? (2) When will it take place? (3) Where will it be held? The Bible is clear that only believers will be present at the Judgment Seat of Christ. It must not be confused with the Great White Throne Judgment (Rev. 20:11-15) at which only the lost will appear. This fact is determined also by the difference in time. The judgment of believers occurs at the coming of the Lord Jesus before the Kingdom age (Matt. 16:27; I Cor. 4:5; I Pet. 1:7; Rev. 22:12), while the judgment of the wicked dead is definitely placed after the Millennium (Rev. 20:6, 7). As to the place where it will be held, we cannot be dogmatic. Since this judgment of the believer's works will take place during the interval between the rapture and the public return of the Lord Jesus to earth, it will take place in the air (I Thess. 4:17). At the close of this period each believer will have passed the inspection of his works, and his appropriate place and rank assigned in the Kingdom reign. Some shall have an abundant entrance (II Pet. 1:11), have confidence at His appearing (I John 2:28), and receive a full reward (II John 8); while others shall be ashamed at His appearing (I John 2:28), and be saved so as by fire (I Cor. 3:15).

These are solemn considerations indeed and to ignore these warnings can only lead to disappointment. No Christian can look with joy to the coming of the Lord while living in known and unconfessed sin. Surely the implications are unmistakable. No wonder Paul says in II Corinthians 5:11,

Knowing therefore the terror of the Lord, we persuade men.

To those who make grace an excuse for careless living, the coming of the Lord cannot be a welcome thought, and many Christians who have thoughtlessly sung, "When by His grace I shall look on His face, That will be glory, be glory for me," are due for a terrible shock when they stand before the Judgment Seat and find that it is not all glory for them, but regrets and remorse at the loss of possible rewards, and being assigned a lower place in the reign of the Kingdom.

The Purpose of the Judgment

We re-emphasize the fact that at the Judgment Seat the believer's salvation and security in Christ will not be the issue. That was settled once for all, but the purpose of this judgment will be to justly reward each servant for work done in the body, on the basis of opportunity and personal ability. Some of the things on which the rewards will be based are:

1. Acts of mercy and love (Luke 6:35, 36).
2. Faithfulness in prayer (Matt. 6:6).
3. Hospitality to the brethren (Matt. 10:42).
4. Motives of our service (Matt. 6:1; I Cor. 4:5).
5. Suffering for Christ (Luke 6:22, 23).
6. Love of His appearing (II Tim. 4:8).
7. Perseverance in well doing (Gal. 6:9).
8. Souls won for Christ (I Thess. 2:19).

To this list others may be added, but these will be some of the things on which rewards will be based in that day.

But Judgment Also

But there is more involved than the gaining or loss of rewards. Most believers have given little thought to what the disapproval of God at the Judgment Seat really means. They are not interested in rewards, but are perfectly content with just being saved and going to heaven. Simply missing a reward or crown holds little dread for them. The reason is failure to see the other side of the Judgment Seat. It not only involves the negative—loss of rewards, but also the positive—"suffering loss" (I Cor. 3:15). It does not say "he shall *enjoy* loss" but *suffer loss*. Certainly the expression, "saved so as by fire," suggests no pleasant or comfortable experience. All the references to God's judgment of believers for unfaithfulness imply something fearful, something to be dreaded and avoided. What else can the words of our Lord mean in Luke 12:47, 48?

> And that servant, which knew his lord's will, and prepared not himself, neither did according to his will, shall be beaten with many stripes.
>
> But he that knew not, and did commit things worthy of stripes, shall be beaten with few stripes.

This is in sharp contrast to the reward of faithful servants of whom Jesus said:

> Blessed is that servant, whom his lord when he cometh shall find so doing.
>
> Of a truth I say unto you, that he will make him ruler over all that he hath (Luke 12:43, 44).

Here we have reward for faithfulness, but the unfaithful servant is to be beaten with stripes, the number of stripes being determined by the amount of light and opportunity which each one possessed. We need not argue about the interpretation or meaning of the "stripes." We may not know the exact nature of the punishment inflicted, but the fact remains that while faithfulness will be rewarded, unfaithfulness will be punished, and the implication is that it will be a painful and humiliating experience.

Thousands of sermons have been preached, and volumes written on the *rewards* and the receiving of *crowns*, but there is little material on the opposite side of the picture, the "loss" of these rewards. It is a significant fact that in Revelation three, after the promise of the believer's escaping the Tribulation, the next verse contains a solemn warning. How comforting the promise in Revelation 3:10,

> Because thou hast kept the word of my patience, I also will keep thee from the hour of temptation, which shall come upon all the world, to try them that dwell upon the earth.

But to stop at verse ten is to miss the important part. Escaping the Tribulation to face the Judgment Seat of Christ unprepared is but meager comfort indeed, and so John adds:

> Behold, I come quickly: hold that fast which thou hast, that no man take thy crown (Rev. 3:11).

Salvation cannot be lost—but rewards and crowns? Yes. Neglect of preaching this side of the Judgment Seat can result in nothing but looseness of conduct, indifference and a false security. If the objection is offered that fear of these consequences is an unworthy motive for faithfulness, we can only reply that if the love of Christ does not constrain us, then God will take a more severe method, for He will have His people clean, "For whom the Lord loveth he chasteneth." This was the great fear in the heart of Paul. He never doubted his salvation, for he could say:

> I know whom I have believed, and am persuaded that he is able to keep that which I have committed unto him against that day (II Tim. 1:12).

Paul did not fear losing his salvation, but he trembled at the thought of losing his crown of reward. One cannot fail to detect Paul's fear of this. Hear him say:

> I therefore so run, not as uncertainly; so fight I, not as one that beateth the air:
> But I keep under my body, and bring it into subjection: lest that by any means, when I have preached to others, I myself should be a castaway (I Cor. 9:26, 27).

The meaning of the word "castaway" had nothing to do with Paul's salvation, but rewards. In the next chapter (I Cor. 10), Paul gives the explanation. Israel was *out* of Egypt forever, but never reached Canaan, their victorious goal, and most of them died! A redeemed people! In the wilderness, short of the land of victory and reward (Heb. 10:4, 5).

THE BASIS OF REWARD

The granting of rewards and the rank in the Kingdom will be on the basis of percentage, and not bulk. The servant who gained only two talents received the same reward as the one who gained five talents, because he had only two to begin with while the other had five (Matt. 25:21,23). Although the one gained only two talents, his percentage was the same as that of the one who gained five — one hundred per cent. But in the case of the pounds (Luke 19:17), the one who gained only five pounds did not receive the same reward as the servant who had gained ten. The reward again was on a percentage basis, for both began with the same amount — one pound (Luke 19:16). The one who gained ten pounds received authority over ten cities, while the other received only five cities. The Lord requires no more from us than we are able to produce, and the reward will be proportionate and just. The principle is clearly stated:

> For unto whomsoever much is given, of him shall be much required: and to whom men have committed much, of him they will ask the more (Luke 12:48).

WHO IS THE JUDGE?

A final word about the Judge, who is none other than the Lord Jesus who gave His all for us. The Lord Himself will be the Judge, and His judgment will take in all the circumstances of our lives, which are hidden from men's eyes, and even hidden from us, and known only to Him. Some believers whom we think were weaklings and failures will be commended by Him, while others whom we have admired for their great success will take a lower place and will receive a lesser reward. In giving these rewards He will not look at our success, but our motive; not the victory but the way in which we fought, even in the hour of defeat; not at what we have accomplished, but how faithful we have been in seeking to accomplish it.

Therefore judge nothing before the time, until the Lord come, who both will bring to light the hidden things of darkness, and will make manifest the counsels of the hearts: and then shall every man have praise of God (I Cor. 4:5).

The M. R. De Haan Classic Library

M. R. De Haan spoke to millions of listeners each week for some twenty-seven years on the *Radio Bible Class* broadcast. His academic training included a degree from Hope College, a medical degree from the University of Illinois Medical College, and further study at Western Theological Seminary. He was the author of more than twenty books and countless daily devotionals in *Our Daily Bread*, published by RBC Ministries of Grand Rapids, Michigan.

Anyone interested in solid biblical studies for personal growth will find these titles to be rich sources of insight and inspiration.

Adventures in Faith: Studies in the Life of Abraham
ISBN 0-8254-2481-x   192 pp.   paperback

Daniel the Prophet
ISBN 0-8254-2475-5   344 pp.   paperback

Pentecost and After: Studies in the Book of Acts
ISBN 0-8254-2482-8   184 pp.   paperback

Portraits of Christ in Genesis
ISBN 0-8254-2476-3   192 pp.   paperback

The Romance of Redemption: Studies in the Book of Ruth
ISBN 0-8254-2480-1   184 pp.   paperback

Studies in First Corinthians
ISBN 0-8254-2478-x   192 pp.   paperback

Studies in Galatians
ISBN 0-8254-2477-1   192 pp.   paperback

Studies in Hebrews
ISBN 0-8254-2479-8   216 pp.   paperback

Available from Christian bookstores or

kregel
PUBLICATIONS

P.O. Box 2607 • Grand Rapids, MI 49501-2607